2024: THE YEAR OF MERCY

17 Prophetic Revelations And 300 Powerful Prayers And Declarations to Command the Year

DANIEL C. OKPARA

WHAT IS GOD SAYING?
POWERFUL PRAYERS AND
DECLARATIONS TO COMMAND
VICTORY AND BREAKTHROUGH
THROUGHOUT THE YEAR

FOLLOW ME ON WHATSAPP

 Follow my channel on WhatsApp. Get powerful daily prayers and testimonies to challenge your faith and command your breakthrough. Search for **Dr. Daniel Okpara** on WhatsApp Updates or Click the link below...

WHATSAPP CHANNEL

https://bit.ly/drdanielokparawhatsapp

Copyright © December 2023 by Daniel C. Okpara.

All Rights Reserved. Kindly note that the contents of this book should not be reproduced in any way or by any means without obtaining written consent from the author or his representative. However, brief excerpts for church or Christian references can be used without written permission.

Published By:

Better Life Media.

BETTER LIFE WORLD OUTREACH CENTER.

Website: www.BetterLifeWorld.org

Email: info@betterlifeworld.org

FOLLOW US ON FACEBOOK

1. FB.com/drdanielokpara

2. Join Our Facebook Prayer Group, submit prayer requests, and follow powerful daily prayers for total victory and breakthrough

Any scripture quotation in this book is taken from the New International Version, New King James Version, except where stated, used by permission.

WAYS TO RECEIVE DAILY AND WEEKLY PRAYERS

1. Subscribe on my website:

www.betterlifeworld.org

2. Follow me on Facebook:

www.facebook.com/drdanielokpara

www.facebook.com/apostledanielokpara

3. Join my WhatsApp Channel:

www.bit.ly/drdanielokparawhatsapp

FREE BOOKS

Download these books for free and take your relationship with God to a new level.

The links are provided at the end of this book.

CONTENTS

FREE BOOKS VI

MY MISSION 9

INTRODUCTION 11

DAY ONE: PROPHETIC WORD #1: THE YEAR OF GRATITUDE 19

DAY TWO: PROPHETIC WORD #2: THE YEAR OF MERCY 31

DAY THREE: PROPHETIC WORD #3: THE YEAR OF A TRANSFORMED HEART 44

DAY FOUR: PROPHETIC WORD #4: THE YEAR OF SACRIFICIAL DEVOTION 51

DAY FIVE: PROPHETIC WORD #5: THE YEAR OF BUILDING THE INNER MAN, INCREASING CAPACITY 62

DAY SIX: PROPHETIC WORD #6: THE YEAR OF HEALING AND RESTORATION 72

DAY SEVEN: PROPHETIC WORD #7: THE YEAR OF COURAGEOUS FAITH 84

DAY EIGHT: PROPHETIC WORD #8: THE YEAR OF NEW DREAMS AND SUPERNATURAL PROVISIONS 97

DAY NINE: PROPHETIC WORD #9: THE YEAR OF THE BLOOD INSURANCE 106

DAY TEN: PROPHETIC WORD #10: THE YEAR OF VICTORY OVER THE FORCES OF DARKNESS 117

DAY ELEVEN: PROPHETIC WORD #11: THE YEAR OF ROYALTY 125

DAY TWELVE: PROPHETIC WORD #12: THE YEAR OF THE FAMILY .. 134

DAY THIRTEEN: PROPHETIC WORD #13: THE YEAR OF RENEWING OF THE MIND 144

DAY FOURTEEN: PROPHETIC WORD #14: THE YEAR OF REALIGNMENT 152

DAY FIFTEEN: PROPHETIC WORD #15: THE YEAR OF THE DECLARER 162

DAY SIXTEEN: PROPHETIC WORD #16: THE YEAR OF ACCEPTABLE OFFERING AND HARVEST 171

DAY SEVENTEEN: DECREE AND DECLARE 182

EPILOGUE: 205

GET IN TOUCH 207

BOOKS BY THE SAME AUTHOR 208

ABOUT THE AUTHOR 211

FREE BOOKS 212

NOTES 213

MY MISSION

God spoke to me in 1998 to write down the things He shows me, that He would use them to set the captives free. I was twenty-one years old then, and that was when I started writing down whatever God showed me in His Word, visions, and dreams.

To the glory of God, we have received thousands of testimonies of salvation, deliverance, and mysterious divine encounters through our books.

Writing is a divine mandate for me. So, as you read this book, *THE YEAR OF MERCY,* expect God's power to manifest beyond your imagination and provoke a turnaround in your life.

DON'T FORGET

"A word from God every day is all you need to build a wall against the enemy's attacks and command miracles in your life."

- Daniel Okpara

INTRODUCTION

Every time we welcome a new year, pundits in all fields add two and two together and come up with what to expect. I do not claim to be one of these gurus. I am a seeker of God with His burden in my soul. God is inspiring my spirit with words and prayers to prepare our hearts, to guide us, and to empower us to ride through the year in victory. This is what I share with you in this book.

Prophetic words are messages inspired by the Holy Spirit to bring reawakening, encouragement, guidance, confirmation, correction, comfort, and divine solutions. The words I have written on these pages are words God put in my heart to encourage you, reassure you of His presence, and provide some confirmation and guidance as you set goals for the new year. As you read, agree, and pray with these words:

- You will have clarity in your decisions.
- Your spirit will be recharged for God.
- You will be convicted and corrected.
- You will repent and be restored.
- You will be strengthened.
- Your gifts and callings will be awakened.
- You will break forth and break through.

Read and receive these words with faith. They are tested with the Holy Scriptures and align with the character and nature of God. They will revive your spirit and empower divine solutions and interventions.

HOW TO USE THIS BOOK

NOTE: Some of the prayers in this book are our yearly prayers, repeated from past editions of our New Year Prayers series. Day 17 is taken from my book, By This Time Tomorrow. These prayers are re-energized to bless you this year.

This book is intended to help you commit seventeen days to prayers and declarations over the new year. Take charge of the year spiritually and dictate its direction. Command the powers of heaven and earth to work in your favor and release all that is rightfully yours.

What is the best month to pray with the book?

In one word: none.

Though I recommend praying with this book in the first quarter of the year, I understand that not everyone will lay hands on the book at the same time. While some may read the book in January, February, or March, others may discover it in June, July, August, September, October, or November.

Whenever you're able to pray with the book is perfectly okay. There's nothing like "If you don't use it around so and so time, the prayers will not work." The main point is to commit to twenty-one days of prayers and speak to the year.

FASTING

I recommend you fast for the seventeen days you commit to the prayers. Fasting empowers us to tame the flesh and build up our spirits. Jesus said that some spiritual issues are resolved only with fasting and prayer (Matthew 17:14- 21 KJV).

What type of fasting is recommended?

If you've read some of my prayer books, I always recommend doing whatever fasting your time, schedule, and health condition can afford. If it is 6-10 or 6-6, that you can do, get on with it.

Choose the nature of fasting that is suitable for you. Day or night fast, none is better than the other.

Some people prefer dinner fast. They skip dinner to pray in the night hours. If that's what is convenient for you, that's great.

The most important thing is for you to understand and commit to a fast while you pray with me in this book.

The only instruction I add to fasting is this: If you feel like or are led to do many days of fasting at a stretch, consider drinking water or juice along.

Remember that our goal in fasting is to humble ourselves before God, not to prove anything or have something to brag about. So, use your fasting to connect to the Spirit, not win an argument.

PRAYER TIMES

Below are the recommended prayer times to pray the prayers in this book:

- 12:00am - 1:00am (Midnight Session)
- 3:00 am - 4:00 am (Early Morning Session)
- 6:00am – 7:00am (Morning Session)
- 12:00 – 1:00 pm (Midday Session)
- 3:00 pm – 4:00 pm (Afternoon Session)
- 9:00 pm – 10:00 pm (Night Session)

You may choose any of these sessions and pray for seventeen days. Whatever fits your schedule is welcome. If you prefer an afternoon session today and a night session tomorrow, it's okay. There are no *must-dos*. The most important thing is to be expectant. Yield to the power of God, and expect a divine turnaround.

May this be a year of peace, joy, breakthrough, favor, and all-around fruitfulness, in Jesus' name.

REMEMBER THIS

"Our goal in fasting is to humble ourselves before God, not to prove anything or have something to brag about."

DAY ONE

PROPHETIC WORD #1

THE YEAR OF GRATITUDE

God is saying to you this year,

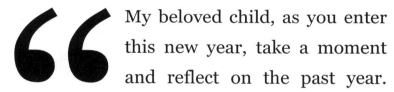My beloved child, as you enter this new year, take a moment and reflect on the past year. Remember the times I showed up for you, provided for your needs, and carried you through difficult moments. Recall the moments of joy and victory. Write them down and give thanks for each one. Your gratitude is a sweet aroma to me.

"Thank me for the mysteries of creation, the beauty surrounding you, and the relationships that bring you joy. Thank me for the lessons you learned in the past year and the growth you experienced. Thank me for the gift of life itself and for every breath you take.

"Perhaps you feel some of your prayers were not answered. Perhaps the wound from the past still lingers in your memory. Maybe the job, marriage, court justice, promotion, or debt cancellation you fervently prayed for still looks farfetched. Nevertheless, recognize that you have every reason to be grateful.

"Even during the hard times, I am always with you, working behind the scenes, arranging everything for your good. I am your protector, your provider, and your guide. And this is my commitment to you: *I will bring beauty out of your ashes*. Your prayers and acts of faith are not in vain.

"Fix your gaze upon me this new year, not on your failures or unanswered prayers. Look beyond your circumstances and focus on my goodness and faithfulness. Ponder on my mighty deeds in your life. Count your blessings and let your heart overflow with praise and worship. I am the source of all blessings, the giver of life, and the one who sustains you.

I AM AT WORK IN YOUR LIFE

"As you enter this year, know that I am at work in your life. Open your heart and be a vessel of gratitude. Go to your space and share about my goodness. Let your praises and thanksgiving resound throughout the channels.

"If you pause a moment and think about the workings of your heart and your life, you will see why you should be grateful. Your heart tirelessly beats, circulating life through your body, pumping blood, and delivering oxygen to sustain every organ and muscle. It beats ceaselessly, a testament to the divine science embedded within your being.

"Imagine if human ingenuity controlled the heartbeat or technology giants dictated its rhythm. The essence of life would become subject to human manipulation.

"My child, recognize that the miracle of life surpasses human mathematics; it is a mystery orchestrated by Me, your heavenly Father. Your heartbeat, the rhythm of life, is sustained not by external forces but by my power.

"Therefore, as long as breath fills your lungs, gratitude is the rightful response. Even in moments of hurt, setbacks, betrayals, and delay, I am actively at work in your life. When you feel my presence and when you don't, when circumstances are favorable and when they are challenging, I, the sustainer of life, am at work in you.

"Pause and ponder the mystery of life and realize that beyond medications and nourishing foods, your Maker's hand provides and empowers the resources sustaining your daily existence.

GRATITUDE CHECK

"Before advancing further, take a moment to reflect on the past year. From January to December, consider my goodness in your life. Find at least twelve blessings I bestowed upon you. Each blessing represents a month of the year. Now, write them down and be grateful."

APPLICATION

1. Remember His Deeds: Shift your focus from unmet needs and challenges to the gratitude check. Recall the past victories, and let faith in His future deliverance arise. As the Psalmist declared, *"I will remember the deeds* of the Lord; yes, I will remember your miracles of long ago."

1. Journal Your Blessing: This year, choose to have a gratitude journal. Set aside time each day to write down at least three things you are grateful for. Reflect on the blessings and goodness of God in your life daily. This practice will help you develop a habit of gratitude and keep your focus on the positive.

2. Be Thankful: Intentionally declare words of gratitude and thanksgiving to God daily. Verbalize your appreciation for His blessings, provision, and faithfulness. Let your words create an atmosphere of gratitude in your surroundings.

3. Share Your Gratitude: Express your gratitude to others. Let your loved ones, friends, colleagues, and social media space know how thankful you are.

4. Be Grateful Even in Challenges: When facing difficulties, intentionally search for the silver linings and lessons. Find something to be grateful for even in the midst of trials. This mindset shift will help you maintain a grateful heart and trust.

5. Be Grateful in Prayers: Prayer is incomplete without gratitude. During prayer times, make thanksgiving and gratitude a significant part of your conversation with God. Start your prayers by expressing thanks, and end your prayers by saying thanks.

6. Share Your Testimonies: For every blessing, deliverance, help, and comfort, share your praise report with others. Remember, there are no small testimonies. Share what God did and inspire someone's faith.

7. Avoid Comparison: Guard your heart against comparison and complaining. Instead of focusing on what others have or what you lack, shift your perspective to gratitude. Count your blessings and celebrate the unique journey God has designed for you.

Immerse yourself in the remembrance of God's faithfulness every day. Meditate on victories and declare faith in His continuous goodness. Let praises burst forth from your soul continually.

PRAYERS

1. Heavenly Father, God of all blessings, source of all life, and giver of all grace. I lift my voice in gratitude for the gift of life, breath, sustenance, family, and community. Your protection and provision in the past year overflow with abundance. As I enter the new year, I declare praise to Your name, in Jesus' name.

2. Father, I thank You for the mystery of creation, the beauty surrounding us, the joy we experience, and the unknown wonders that captivate our hearts. Thank You for the vastness of the universe, the mystery of communities, and the establishment of family and friendships. Every aspect of life draws us into awe, and for this, I offer unending thanks in Jesus' name.

3. O LORD, thank You for this day, this year, and the opportunity to experience Your love again. For everything You have done, are doing, and will do, I give thanks to You, in Jesus' name.

4. I praise You, O Lord, for Your mighty acts of deliverance. You saved us, protected us, and provided for us. Your love and kindness endure daily, and I thank You for Your constant care. You did not despise my cries but listened and

helped me throughout the year. My praise will continually be unto You, in Jesus' name.

5. *PSALM 138:1-3:* "O Lord, our God, maker of heaven and earth. You are the Lord God Almighty. Your praise and glory fill the earth and my life and family. I thank You, Lord, with all my heart.

6. Today, I sing praise to You before the gods. I face Your holy Temple, bow down, and praise Your name because of Your constant love and faithfulness. You answered me when I called to You; Your strength strengthened me. May Your name be praised forever and ever, in Jesus' name.

7. O LORD, though You are high above, You care for the lowly. In troubles, You keep me safe, oppose my enemies, and save me with Your power. You will fulfill every promise and complete the work You have begun in me. Be

glorified forever and ever, in Jesus' name. Amen.

8. Thank You, LORD, for being my ever-present help in times of trouble and for turning my trials into triumphs. Thank You for the divine connections and appointments You orchestrated in my life. Thank You for the doors that You opened and the opportunities You have presented to me. Thank You for the favor and blessings that flow from You.

9. I am grateful for the gift of salvation through Jesus Christ. I am thankful for the abundant provisions in my life. I am grateful for the talents and abilities God has given me.

10. I am thankful for the peace and joy that come from God. In this Year of Gratitude, I will count my blessings daily and declare God's goodness and faithfulness, in Jesus' name.

MEDITATION

1 Chronicle 16:34 - Oh, give thanks to the Lord, for He is good! For His mercy endures forever

Colossians 3:17 - And whatever you do, whether in word or deed, do it all in the name of the Lord Jesus, giving thanks to God the Father through him.

Ephesians 5:20 - Always giving thanks to God the Father for everything, in the name of our Lord Jesus Christ.

Psalm 95:2 - Let us come before him with thanksgiving and extol him with music and song.

2 Corinthians 9:15 - Thanks be to God for his indescribable gift!

DAY TWO

PROPHETIC WORD #2

THE YEAR OF MERCY

Thus says the LORD,

"Behold, I am opening the doors of mercy upon the earth this year. I am opening the doors of reconciliation and healing. By My mercy, I am canceling judgment and birthing new hope. Those who embrace My mercy and turn to Me will not face judgment. But those who ignore and rebel will be left on their own.

"This year, I am extending My hand to the brokenhearted, the weary, the lost, and the suffering. I am reaching out to those who have wandered far from Me, to those burdened by guilt and shame. My mercy knows no limits, and I am releasing it in abundance this year.

"Release the weight of fear, condemnation, and shame in your heart. I set before you a river of compassion. Run to it, wash yourself from every stain, and restore your soul.

"I am the God of second chances; this is the year of My mercy canceling judgment. I do not hold onto your errors, mistakes, failures, and sins. I do not remember what you did wrong and what you could have done better.

"Come to Me confidently; I am ready to receive you with open arms. I forgive the repentant, wipe their tears, and heal their wounds. It's time to stop counting your mistakes and start counting your blessings. It's time to stop focusing on the opinions and judgments of men about you and focus on My mercy. No matter how far you have fallen or missed it, it is not over with you. I am reconciling you back to Myself, giving you a new beginning, and empowering you to bounce back better. Allow My mercy to be a balm to your brokenness, a soothing salve that brings wholeness and renewal.

"Receive My mercy and extend it to others this year. Remember, *blessed are the merciful, for they shall obtain mercy.* As you receive My mercy, go out and be an instrument of mercy in the world. Let your words and actions reflect My compassion, kindness, and forgiveness.

"Be a source of hope and restoration to those around you. Start a mercy project and reach out to those wounded in spirit, soul, and body. Allow me to use you and bring a smile to the suffering and broken. The world can only see My mercy when you and my other children step out and show them mercy.

"Pray for the nations. Declare My mercy over them. Stand in the gap and call their hearts to repentance. My mercy will break chains of bondage, dismantle strongholds, and transform individuals, communities, and systems. My mercy will triumph over judgment and activate mending and healing seasons.

"Receive the year of My mercy with faith and expectation, for I am doing a new thing in your life and in the world. Let My mercy be your guiding light, leading you into a deeper intimacy with Me and a greater manifestation of My love in and through you."

APPLICATION

This year will be marked by an outpouring of God's mercy, grace, and compassion. Many who have felt distant from God or burdened by guilt and shame will experience His forgiveness and restoration. Divine interventions and breakthroughs will occur as God's mercy intervenes in seemingly impossible situations.

Individuals and nations will have opportunities to turn away from destructive paths and embrace love. Acts of kindness, generosity, and compassion will increase, fostering a sense of unity and harmony among people. God will show mercy to the marginalized, oppressed, and forgotten.

The body of Christ will play a vital role in extending God's mercy to the world. Charities and structures from the Church will demonstrate Christ's love through practical acts of service and compassion. There will be an emphasis on forgiveness and reconciliation, personally and collectively.

God's mercy will also extend to the environment, inspiring efforts to protect and preserve the natural world. Individuals and communities will experience a sense of peace and joy as they embrace God's mercy.

Remember that while this prophetic word provides a glimpse into the year's blessings, you have a role to play.

1. Receive His mercy: Receive God's mercy with open arms and let go of guilt, shame, and condemnation. Allow His forgiveness to wash over you, and experience the freedom and restoration that come with His mercy.

2. Extend His mercy: Be a vessel of God's mercy to others. Show compassion, kindness, and forgiveness to those around you. Let your words and actions reflect His love and grace. Start projects of mercy in your neighborhood or community. God's mercy extends to the nations through His children.

3. Pray for the nations: Lift up the nations in prayer, asking God to pour out His mercy and bring transformation. Pray for repentance, reconciliation, and the breaking of chains of bondage. Pray for abandoned children, the wounded, the suffering, and the rejected.

PRAYERS

1. Heavenly Father, I humble myself before You today and surrender to Your Authority and Power.

2. I plead that Your mercy will speak for me in every area of my life this year.

3. By Your mercy, deliver me from the consequences of all my errors and sins.

4. By Your mercy, protect me from the evil one and from the evil world.

5. By Your mercy, inspire and guide me toward righteousness and holiness.

6. By Your mercy, let your army of angels take over all my battles.

7. By Your mercy, grant me peace that passes human comprehension.

8. By Your mercy, heal my soul and deliver me from pain, brokenness, disappointments, and delays.

9. By Your mercy, connect me with the partner You have for me.

10. By Your mercy, deliver me from shame and near breakthrough syndrome.

11. By Your mercy, show me things I do not know, things about my life that I should commit to, and bring glory to Your name.

12. By your mercy, protect my marriage from strange women and men.

13. By Your mercy, connect me with my destiny helpers.

14. By Your mercy, empower me with ideas for financial breakthroughs.

15. By Your mercy, deliver our land from bloodshed, terrorism, bitterness, and anger.

16. By Your mercy, protect and preserve my family from destroyers.

17. By Your mercy, let every curse, enchantment, charm, and witchcraft against my life and destiny be permanently erased and destroyed.

18. By Your mercy, let every persistent enemy with the spirit of Pharaoh, Herod, and Jezebel, chasing my life and destiny, drown in the spiritual red sea of life.

19. By Your mercy, grant me favor with people and bless the works of my hands.

20. By Your mercy, open doors for me to fulfill Your assignment for my life.

21. Pour out Your mercy upon every nation, from the east to the west and from the north to the south.

22. By Your mercy, end wars, conflicts, and violence that plague the nations.

23. By Your mercy, replace hatred with love, division with unity, and injustice with justice. Let Your mercy prevail and usher in a season of peace and reconciliation.

24. By Your mercy, provide for the needs of nations facing poverty, famine, and hardships.

25. By Your mercy, inspire solutions to alleviate suffering, empower neighborhoods, and uplift the downtrodden.

26. By Your mercy, inspire sustainable development and prosperity.

27. By Your mercy, heal the nations from the ravages of diseases, wars, and pandemics.

28. By Your mercy, grant wisdom to scientists, researchers, and healthcare professionals seeking cures and treatments.

29. By Your mercy, heal the sick and grieving. Restore health and wholeness to people and communities.

30. By Your mercy, dismantle oppressive governments and systems. Overturn injustice and corruption that hinder the progress and security of nations.

31. By Your mercy, raise leaders who govern with integrity, wisdom, and compassion.

32. By Your mercy, shield lives and properties from destruction and provide strength and resilience to the affected.

33. By Your mercy, let the gospel of Jesus Christ spread throughout the nations, bringing hope, salvation, and transformation to all who hear it.

34. By Your mercy, let the chains of spiritual bondage and idolatry that hold nations captive be broken. Let there be a great awakening to people's hearts, leading them to experience spiritual revival.

34. By Your mercy, guide the leaders of nations. Grant them wisdom and compassion as they make decisions that impact the lives of their citizens.

35. By Your mercy, inspire dialogue between nations, different cultures, religions, and ideologies; in Jesus' name, I pray.

Amen.

MEDITATION

Psalm 103:8 – *The LORD is merciful and gracious, slow to anger and abounding in steadfast love* (ESV).

DAY THREE

PROPHETIC WORD #3

THE YEAR OF A TRANSFORMED HEART

God is saying to you this year,

"My child, this is a year of a transformed heart. I desire a new version of you in the world. Allow Me to work inside you and remove what is not of Me. Just as every creator upgrades their software to meet with changing times, I desire to install a new you for the times ahead. I want to purify and wash away any impurities hindering your intimacy with Me. Surrender your heart before Me every day this year, and let Me work on it. I will remove the stains of guilt, shame, fear, and anxiety.

"I will create in you a clean heart that beats in rhythm with Mine. I will fill you with My faith and perspective. I will release a renewed steadfastness within you, a spirit that remains firm despite the challenges and distractions that will come your way.

"My child, ask Me to breathe new life into the depths of your being. I will heal your wounds and restore your brokenness. I will infuse in you a fresh passion, faith, and zeal. Then, you will experience an overflow of love, joy, and peace. Your relationships will be transformed. Your words will carry the power of life, and your actions will reflect My will."

APPLICATION

Until we are transformed within, we cannot be changed without. Every breakthrough begins on the inside. So, God is calling you to a deep heart transformation this year. Cry out to Him as David did in Psalm 51:10: *"Create in me a clean heart, O God, and renew a steadfast spirit within me."*

This will involve a radical renewal of the mind to weed out every seed not planted by God. The fears must pack and leave. The unbelief must wither. The bitterness must be uprooted.

Declare with conviction that this is the year of renewal. Ask the Holy Spirit to renew Your heart and expose any sin and stronghold fighting your destiny. A new version of you must emerge this year, in Jesus' name.

PRAYERS

1. Heavenly Father, I come before You today and surrender my heart completely to You. I ask for Your power to cleanse, purify, and wash away any impurities and sins hindering my

intimacy with You. Remove the stains of sin, guilt, shame, fear, and anxiety from my heart, in Jesus' name.

2. O LORD, I give You my heart each day this year. Through Your Spirit, work on me and transform me according to Your will. Create in me a clean heart that beats in perfect rhythm with Your own, in Jesus' name.

3. Father, fill me with Your faith and perspective all through this year. Help me to see the world through Your eyes and trust in Your goodness and sovereignty. Teach and empower me to remain firm in the face of challenges and distractions, in Jesus' name.

4. Holy Spirit, breathe new life into the depths of my being. Heal my wounds and restore my brokenness. Infuse me with fresh passion, faith, and zeal for service this year, and cause

Your love, joy, and peace to overflow in my life, in Jesus' name.

5. This year, Father, empower and transform my relationships. May Your love and grace flow through me and touch the lives of those around me. May my words carry the power of life, encouragement, and truth. May my actions reflect Your will and bring glory to Your name, in the mighty name of Jesus Christ.

6. I declare that this is the year of renewal and transformation in my life. Holy Spirit, renew my heart and expose any sin or stronghold that hinders me from experiencing divine favor, mercy, help, and interventions. Help me let go of my fears, doubts, and bitterness, in Jesus' name.

7. Holy Spirit, weed out every seed not planted by You in my heart. Remove unbelief and replace it with faith in Your promises. Uproot

bitterness or unforgiveness and fill me with Your love and forgiveness, in Jesus' name.

8. Thank You, Father, for the opportunity to be transformed this year. I know that every breakthrough begins on the inside. Therefore, I ask that You help me to embrace this process wholeheartedly and trust in You without comparing myself to others, in Jesus' name.

9. Father, let there be heart transformation in me this year. Create a clean heart, and renew a steadfast spirit within me. May my thoughts, desires, and intentions align with Your Word and purposes, in Jesus' name.

10. I declare that a new version of me will emerge this year. I will be a vessel of honor, transmitting God's love, light, and grace and impacting the world around me, in Jesus' name.

MEDITATION

Psalm 51: 10 - *Create in me a clean heart, O God, and renew a steadfast spirit within me.*

DAY FOUR

PROPHETIC WORD #4

THE YEAR OF SACRIFICIAL DEVOTION

Thus says the LORD,

"My child, this is not just a year to turn the calendar; it is a portal to a realm of purpose. It is a year I am calling you for sacrificial devotion and commitment.

"No longer will half-hearted gestures and lukewarm faith suffice. This year demands a fire in your belly, a love that burns bright and fierce, and a dedication that transcends mere words.

"It is time to lay your heart upon the altar, not of obligation, but of willing surrender, knowing that in this sacrifice lies the greatest gain.

"Three pillars shall guide your path in this year of devotion:

1. Seek to Know Thy Purpose: Pursue not comfort but clarity. Query the uneasiness in your spirit. Unbundle the vision that stirs your soul. Dive deep within, silence the clamor of the world, and listen to the whisper of your purpose. It may not be majestic or trendy, but it will resonate with your authentic self. Hold on to it, and let it be your compass.

2. Allow the Refinement Process: The path of devotion is not paved with roses. Expect challenges, doubt, and moments of searing fire. These are not obstacles but crucibles in which your commitment is forged into unyielding steel. Embrace the challenges that will come;

they will shred away the waste and reveal the pure gold within. Let your faith be your furnace, your resolve, your hammer, and your spirit, the unyielding anvil.

3. Commit to Service: True devotion is not a solitary dance. It spills over into the lives of others. This year, be a vessel of service; pour your gifts and talents into others. Seek not recognition, but the quiet satisfaction of a life lived in service. In serving, you shall receive blessings beyond measure, for the LORD rewards those who selflessly contribute to the fabric of life.

"Remember, my child, this is not a year for the faint of heart. It is a year for the audacious, the untiring, and those who choose to dance on the edge of possibility. Step into this year with a warrior's spirit, a lover's heart, and a servant's hand. Let your devotion be your armor, your commitment your compass, and your service your legacy. This is the year you rise, not just above your circumstances but into the fullness of your potential.

"Go forth, My child, and make this year a testament to your sacrificial devotion and commitment. Offer your life as a living sacrifice, holy and pleasing to Me. Lay down your desires, ambitions, and plans at My feet. Let Me be the center of your affections and the source of your strength. Walk in radical obedience and wholehearted commitment.

"Prepare to make sacrifices for My sake and for the advancement of My Kingdom. Embrace the cost and be willing to go the extra mile. I reveal Myself to those who seek Me diligently. I will release a grace upon you to deny yourself, take up your cross daily, and follow Me. As you align your priorities with Mine, I will pour out My favor and blessings upon you. Your devotion and commitment will be rewarded with divine encounters, supernatural provision, and an outpouring of My Spirit."

APPLICATION

This year, as you plan, lay down your desires, ambitions, and plans at His feet. Seek His will. Choose His leading, radical obedience, and fervent commitment.

Be willing to make sacrifices for the sake of the Kingdom and the visions expanded in your spirit. Pray more in the spirit with the Word as a guide. Be open to divine encounters and write down every dream, vision, and instruction He gives you.

Be faithful and resolute in your devotion and divine commitments no matter the challenges that come. Walk in the power of the Holy Spirit, and allow His presence to manifest in your life. Know that God will reward your sacrificial devotion.

PRAYERS

1. Heavenly Father, I thank You once again for this year. Thank You for calling me to a higher consecration and dedication to You. Thank You for Your grace and mercy that makes it possible, in Jesus' name.

2. O LORD, I answer Your call with a wholehearted yes. I willingly offer myself to You and lay all on the altar of consecration – my time, talents, desires, and dreams. Take complete control, and let Your will be done in my life. May I be a living sacrifice, holy and acceptable to You. Take full control of my life and use me for Your glory, in Jesus' name.

3. Father, fill me with Your Spirit and empower me to live a life pleasing before You this year. Help me to die to self and live for Christ. Help me to mortify the flesh and walk in the Spirit. Help me to renounce the world and seek Your

kingdom. Help me to resist the devil and submit to Your authority. Help me to carry the cross and follow Your will. I surrender my plans and ambitions to You. Help me to trust Your ways, even when they seem uncertain or challenging, in Jesus' name.

4. Holy Spirit, help me to endure the testing and refining process. Purify me as gold and silver are purified in the fire. Remove any impurities and trash that are not pleasing to You. Prune me and cut off any branch that does not bear fruit. I dedicate my relationships to You. May they be built on the foundation of love and mutual respect. Deliver and heal me from any toxic relationships that are attacking my commitment, devotion, and service, in Jesus' name.

5. I declare that this is a year of sacrificial devotion and commitment. Holy Spirit, help me to bear fruit for Your glory. Make me a

vessel of honor. Make me a faithful and loyal servant. Make me willing and obedient. Make me a passionate and zealous follower of You. Help me to make You the center of my affections and to seek Your will above everything else. I lay down my desires, ambitions, and plans at Your feet. Remove whatever is not of You and fill my desires with Your desires, in Jesus' name.

6. Father, I declare that I am willing to make sacrifices for the sake of the Kingdom. Show me how to lay down my life for You and others this year. Give me a generous and selfless heart. I surrender my finances to Your LORDSHIP. Teach me to steward them wisely and use them for divine purposes. May my giving reflect my commitment to You, in Jesus' name.

7. Jehovah Rohi, the LORD, my Shepherd, align my priorities with Yours this year. Help me to please You and live a life that brings glory

to Your name. Open my eyes to see Your direction and hear Your voice through Your Word. Draw me closer to You through prayer, fasting, and meditation. Help me to know You intimately and walk in Your wisdom, in Jesus' name.

8. Father, I declare divine encounters and supernatural provision in my life this year. Open my eyes to see Your hand in my circumstances. Even in challenging times, help me to be faithful and persistent in my consecration and commitment, in Jesus' name.

9. LORD, Jesus Christ, I surrender my comfort zone to You this year. Empower me to step out in faith and embrace the unknown for Your glory. Help me to stand firm and persevere in my faith. Help me to overcome fear and hesitation. May my commitment lead to divine breakthroughs in every area of my life, in Jesus' name.

10. Holy Spirit, as I lay my life on the altar and seek Your face this year, I ask for a fresh anointing and favor. Let Your glory fill every area of my existence. May the secret cries of my heart open doors of blessings and opportunities that only You can provide, in Jesus' name.

MEDITATION

Romans 12:1-2 – I beseech you therefore, brethren, by the mercies of God, that you present your bodies a living sacrifice, holy, acceptable to God, which is your reasonable service (NKJV).

DAY FIVE

PROPHETIC WORD #5

THE YEAR OF BUILDING THE INNER MAN, INCREASING CAPACITY

God is saying to you today,

"My child, hear the whisper of eternity in the silence of your soul. This year is not a race for recognition but a pilgrimage to the depths of your spirit. Turn your gaze inward, for the most incredible adventure awaits within. This is a year of praying in the Holy Spirit, building the inner man, strengthening your roots, developing capacity, and preparing for the breakthroughs ahead.

"This year, My child, forget the shallow echoes of self-help, the empty rituals of religion, the cry for applause, the strong urge for validation, the chase for fleeting trends, and the trap of societal expectations. Step into the sanctuary of the Holy Spirit. Let His breath fill your lungs, His fire cleanse your soul, and His whispers guide your actions. Embrace Spirit-led prayer, intercession, and self-discovery.

"Seek not to be known, but to know. Seek not to be validated but to be led. Seek not to meet societal expectations but to be approved by Me, a workman who cannot be ashamed. Your version from yesterday cannot accommodate what I have in store for you in the future. This is why I charge you to ignite the fire of your spirit through much praying in tongues. Increase your faith to receive. See beyond your present. Unmask your true self, and develop a lion demeanor.

"As you yield your heart and pray in the Holy Spirit, the mysteries of heaven are unveiled, and breakthroughs are released. Your gifts are empowered, and your desires aligned with Mine. Your fears and anxieties are trashed, and your authority is unleashed.

"In the hustle and bustle of this year, My child, carve out a space for stillness. Seek the sanctuary of silence. Feed on My Word. Meditate, journal, commune with nature, and pray in tongues. My Spirit will transform you, renew your mind, heal your deep wounds, align your actions, and unleash you as a force.

"I am raising a generation of warriors who will impact nations through their stories and testimonies. You are among this generation. Therefore, prepare yourself for the assignments and opportunities I have for you. Build up your most holy faith; grow in the inner man and equip the warrior within.

"Pray much in unknown tongues. Let the fire of the Holy Spirit speak through you, unlocking depths and mysteries and forging a deep connection with heavenly authority.

"Increase your capacity. Invest in yourself, know your gifts, develop them, and expand your vessel to receive My blessings.

"Feed your inner man. The enemy is after your faith, so don't leave your faith to chance. An unfed faith will die a natural death. Just as your body needs nourishment, your spirit and faith need the right food to stay healthy."

APPLICATION

Build up your most holy faith by praying much in tongues. Nurture a lifestyle of praying and worshipping in tongues this year. Allow the Holy Spirit to guide your words, sounds, and declarations in prayers. He will inspire your heart and fill you with unique thoughts. He will convict you and correct you. He will expose areas in your life that need attention and surrender.

Develop a posture of listening to the LORD. Be attentive to His promptings throughout the day. Walk by faith, not by sight. As you pray in the Holy Spirit, you'll develop capacity, empower the warrior within you, and grow the inner man, fit and ready for God's use.

Also, seek opportunities for personal growth and development, both in your spiritual walk and in skills that align with your calling. Be humble and teachable. Seek to know, not to be known. Growth requires a willingness to learn and be molded by the Holy Spirit.

PRAYERS

1. Heavenly Father, in this year of building the inner man, praying in the Holy Spirit, and building capacity, I yield myself to Your Spirit's

guidance. Empower me to pray in tongues fervently and unlock mysteries and strategies for fulfilling Your purpose for my life. Let my prayers be a powerful force for breakthroughs in my life and in the lives of others, in Jesus' name.

2. Holy Spirit, ignite my spirit as I pray in the Spirit. Align my prayers with Your perfect will and release breakthroughs and revelations as I yield to Your leading, in Jesus' name.

3. In the name of Jesus Christ, I turn my gaze inward and embrace a Spirit-led prayer and intercession this year. As I pray in the Holy Spirit daily, my gifts will be empowered, and my actions will be aligned with God's perfect will. I will walk in the authority of Christ and be a testimony of His transformation, in Jesus' name.

4. O LORD, increase my faith to receive all You have in store for me. Help me to see beyond my present circumstances and ignite the fire of my spirit. Develop within me a lion-like demeanor that overcomes fear and embraces my divine destiny, in Jesus' name.

5. Holy Spirit, amid this year's hustle and bustle, help me carve out a space for stillness. Empower me to seek the sanctuary of silence, feed on Your Word, meditate, journal, commune with nature, and pray in tongues. Transform me, renew my mind, heal my wounds, and align my actions with Yours, in Jesus' name.

6. I declare that I am part of the generation of warriors raised by God to impact nations through my stories and testimonies. I surrender myself to the divine training required for the assignments and opportunities He has for me. I yield my spirit to be equipped

and empowered for the breakthroughs that lie ahead of me, in Jesus' name.

7. Holy Spirit, from this day onwards, take over my prayer and worship times. Guide my words, sounds, and declarations in prayer. Inspire my heart, convict and correct me, and constantly expose areas that need attention and surrender every day. As I worship, sing, and pray in tongues, increase my capacity, charge the warrior within me, and prepare me for God's use, in Jesus' name.

8. Father, enlarge my heart to carry more of Your presence and power this year. Increase my faith and empower me to walk in greater authority and effectiveness, in Jesus' name.

9. O LORD, I surrender to the leading of the Holy Spirit this year. Fill me with the courage to face my shadows, the wisdom to learn from them, and the love to embrace myself fully.

Empower me to do the good works You have called me to do before the foundation of this world, in Jesus' name.

10. Holy Spirit, position and lead me into supernatural encounters to accelerate my spiritual growth. Open my eyes to see and my ears to hear what You are saying in this season. As I press into heaven's mysteries, may Your glory be revealed in my life, and may I reflect the image of Christ more and more, in Jesus' name.

MEDITATION

Jude 1:20 – But you, beloved, building yourselves up in your most holy faith and praying in the Holy Spirit (ESV).

DAY SIX

PROPHETIC WORD #6

THE YEAR OF HEALING AND RESTORATION

God is saying to you this year,

" My beloved child, I see the weight you have carried for far too long, the burdens that have left you weary and broken. Listen closely, for this is the year of healing and restoration. This is the year where longstanding afflictions will give way to My intervention, and every brokenness transformed into wholeness. You will step into My healing streams and experience My restoration power in every area of your life. The weight you have carried for months, years, or even decades will be removed.

"In this year, physical ailments that have plagued you will be confronted by My healing power. Chronic pain will give way to strength. Incurable diseases will bow to the name of Jesus Christ. Wounded hearts will be healed and mended. The scars of past trauma, grief, and broken relationships will be touched by the gentle hand of the Great Physician. I will bring profound healing to your spirit, soul, and body.

"The dry places in your soul will be drenched with the refreshing rain of the Holy Spirit. Spiritual hunger will be awakened, and the fire of passion will be rekindled. The chains of spiritual bondage will be shattered, and a new level of intimacy will be installed.

"Just as I encountered the man at the pool of Mercy, I am reaching out to touch the afflicted areas of your life. Visualize the scene: a pool called Bethesda, surrounded by five entrances, where the sick lay waiting. Just as the waters of Bethesda awaited the stirring of an angel, so too do the still waters within your soul yearn for a divine disruption. You have been waiting, longing for change, but now is the time to rise from the waters of stagnation and embrace My healing move in your spirit.

"I am the God of healing and restoration. This year, I am stirring the waters of Mercy in your life, causing the healing springs to flow. Get ready to be immersed in the refreshing flow of My Spirit as I bring forth supernatural healing and restoration.

"Be honest with yourself about the areas of your life that need help and healing and embrace the divine stirs by faith. Identify the hurts, disappointments, and brokenness that have taken abode in the depths of your being, and surrender them to Me. Allow my light to illuminate those hidden corners and bring deep healing to those wounded places.

"Remember, as you journey through this stirring, you may remember the neglect, the rejection, and the abandonment of the past. You may experience resurfacing emotions such as grief, anger, and fear. You may be tempted to make excuses, preventing yourself from rising and taking a step of faith. You may have genuine reasons to resist change and stick with the norm. But trust Me when I say to you, *"Rise. Take up your bed and walk."*

"Just as I commanded the man to rise, take up his bed, and go home, I command you to rise above your limitations this year. Command the chains that have bound you to fall off. Claim my healing touch and enter a new season of movement and freedom.

"My beloved, I am the Redeemer of lost years, the One who restores what was stolen. In this year, I will bring forth the restoration of what was lost. I will redeem the time you thought was wasted. Position yourself for an encounter. Declare my word. Pray in the Spirit. Step up and step out by faith. Start sharing with others my goodness. Let your testimony ignite hope and confidence in the hearts of others. Remember, whenever you make healing happen in someone else's life, you bring your healing closer.

APPLICATION

The word for today is from the healing story in John 5:1-8. Just as Jesus encountered the man at the pool of Bethesda, this is the year when God will visit those afflicted with longstanding infirmities. Like the man who had suffered for thirty-eight years, many of us carry heavy issues that have persisted for far too long. But the Master Healer is drawing near. He is reaching out His hand to touch those areas marked by pain and brokenness.

The pool of Bethesda symbolizes the mercy, healing, and restoration that God desires to release in our lives. Just as an angel stirred the waters of Bethesda, so will the healing waters of God's Spirit be stirred in your spirit. Prepare to immerse yourself in the refreshing flow of His divine intervention.

1. Rise, take up your bed, and walk: Jesus commanded the man to rise, take up his bed, and walk; so too is the Master calling you to rise and cast off the weight of hopelessness. Receive His healing Word, rise, and enter a new season of freedom.

2. Restoration of lost years: The man at the pool spent years in affliction and missed thousands of opportunities. Yet, when Jesus encountered him, restoration and redemption came forth. Likewise, God will redeem the lost years in this year of healing and restoration. What was taken will be returned, and what was broken will be made whole.

3. Position yourself: As you pray, worship, and declare the Word daily, you position yourself for a divine encounter. So, intensify your Word confession, not your problem confession, this year.

4. Don't focus on the past: When Jesus asked the man, "Do you want to be made well?" he explained how he had missed opportunities and how no one wanted to help him. This year, don't count the losses and missed opportunities. Don't blame anyone. Focus on what Christ is doing in your life, and receive His healing power.

5. Exercise faith: Just as the man had to exercise faith by rising, taking up his bed, and walking, take steps of faith in response to God's healing touch. As you respond to His call, expect to witness the manifestation of His promise.

6. Be patient with yourself: Your healing is happening, even if it's not instant. There may be times when progress feels slow or old wounds resurface, but do not lose heart. God is with you every step of the way, guiding you toward complete wholeness.

PRAYERS

1. Heavenly Father, I thank You for the prophetic word that this is a year of healing and restoration. I receive it by faith and declare that Your healing power is at work in my life, restoring every sick area, in Jesus' name.

2. O LORD, I surrender my brokenness and pain to You. Heal the scars of the past and mend the broken wings of my heart. I receive Your tender touch and believe You are making all things new, according to Your promises, in Jesus' name.

3. Father, I choose to forgive myself and others. I release any bitterness, resentment, or unforgiveness that has hindered my healing and restoration. By Your grace, I embrace the freedom that comes from forgiveness and walk in the light of Your love, in Jesus' name.

4. I declare that my healing will happen, and I will experience a complete restoration in every area of my life, in Jesus' name.

5. My Heavenly Father, I choose to focus on gratitude this day and year. Even in challenges, I acknowledge Your goodness and faithfulness. Thank You for Your presence, provision, and

the countless blessings You have bestowed upon me. Fill my heart with gratitude and joy, in Jesus' name.

6. LORD Jesus, I ask for divine encounters and opportunities to share my story of healing and restoration. Use my testimony to encourage and inspire others on their own journeys. Let Your light shine through me as a beacon of hope and a testament to Your healing power, in Jesus' name.

7. Holy Spirit, I ask for divine wisdom and discernment as I navigate this year of healing and restoration. Guide my steps and align my will with Yours. Help me to make choices that reflect Your health and restoration plan and bring glory to Your name, in Jesus' name.

8. Thank You, Father, for Your promises of healing, restoration, renewal, redemption, and transformation. I declare that Your Word has

power; I hold onto these promises with faith, in Jesus' name.

9. O LORD, I surrender my fears, doubts, and insecurities to You. Fill me with Your peace that surpasses all understanding. Strengthen my faith and grant me the courage to embrace the journey of healing and restoration You have set before me, in Jesus' name.

10. In the name of Jesus Christ, I declare that I am stepping into God's healing streams. I am receiving my healing and restoration. I am rising, walking, and sharing my testimony this year, in Jesus' name.

MEDITATION

Jeremiah 30:17 - For I will restore health to you, and your wounds I will heal, declares the Lord (ESV).

DAY SEVEN

PROPHETIC WORD #7

THE YEAR OF COURAGEOUS FAITH

God is saying to you today,

"My child, this is a year to walk in courageous faith — a faith that defies obstacles and sticks its hold on My Word. It is a year to walk in *the Davidic faith* and refuse to be intimidated by the size of the giant that shows up in your life.

"As you step out to live your full life and change the visible realities of your existence, you will encounter crushing challenges and obstacles. However, do not be discouraged by the size or intensity of the battles, refusals, and failures that arise. Instead, shift your perspective and see every one of them as an opportunity for Me to demonstrate My power in your life.

"Just as David saw an opportunity to fulfill his dream of joining the military through the Goliath situation, know that there are hidden opportunities within every battle. As you walk in faith, the Holy Spirit will open your eyes to the benefits and possibilities hidden inside each situation.

"This year, My child, where others see a problem, see an opportunity for growth, promotion, and victory. Let your perspective be rooted in My Word and in the understanding that I am greater than any obstacle or giant you face. Reject the voices of fear, impossibility, and despair that will try to attack your mind. Charge at those hidden voices and replace every fear, anxiety, and discouragement with trust, courage, and boldness. Your faith in My ability to turn obstacles into opportunities will pave the way for breakthrough and success.

"I declare to you, beloved, that no giant will be too big to conquer, and no challenge will be insurmountable this year. Your courageous faith will position you for divine opportunities, and you will see the manifestation of My power and provision in your life. Your outlook of faith will transform obstacles into stepping stones and lead you to new levels of victory."

APPLICATION

Faith is acting on the word of God inspired or revealed in your heart. It's not complicated, especially when you remove all the theological jargon.

When God inspires a wisdom, an idea, a step, a direction, a judgment, a prayer – anything - in your heart, while in prayers, personal study, or deep reflection, you get up and act on it. If things don't work out as expected, you return to the word and act on it repeatedly. That's faith.

> ***Without faith, we will suffer the same tortures others are suffering.***

Highlight that statement. Copy it somewhere and memorize it. Without faith, nothing works. Without faith, we will not be healed. Without faith, we will not prosper. And without faith, we will not be protected.

God told Moses, "I will effect your deliverance tonight. Tell the Israelites to kill a lamb and paste its blood on their doorposts. That way, they'll be safe."

Imagine if Moses said, "Yes, sir." And then does nothing. After all, there was no way to be sure what would happen.

Imagine if they didn't act on the word.

They could have said, "O God, you can protect us. You have the power. Why let us go through this sort of stress? Please, just protect us."

But thank God they didn't act in unbelief. Moses spoke to them, telling them what to do. They listened and acted on the word. That's walking by faith and not by sight. Consequently, they were preserved from the angel of death.

God will preserve you and your household from the angel of violence this year, in Jesus' name.

Nevertheless, you must choose faith over fear. When anxiety and fear strike, challenge them with faith. Declare the Word and never accept anything contrary.

Those who don't mix the word with faith don't see its manifestation. Without faith, the Word will not work.

> **Hebrews 4:2** - For unto us was the gospel preached, as well as unto them: but the word preached did not profit them, not being mixed with faith in them that heard it.

Sometimes, the doctors will give you a diagnosis that doesn't sound good. But you must look up the *Word* of God about your health and stick with what it says, not the diagnosis.

Being in the covenant does not mean we will not see the problems in the nation. It does not mean that God will cuddle us every morning and shout from the sky, saying, *"Dan, go and greet Mr Peter and tell him to give you a thousand dollars."*

No, we will have problems and also see the issues in the world. But we must walk in the assurance that we are already empowered and marked by the Blood of the Lamb. We must walk by faith, not by sight. If not, we will become victims of what is affecting others.

If you see deaths and disasters around you, you keep saying, "I shall not die; I dwell in the secret place of the Most High."

If there is increased famine in your country, you continue to say, "My case is different. I shall not lack. God will supply all my needs according to His riches in Christ."

If you hear a negative medical report, you keep saying, "God is with me. My health is getting better every day. Jesus took my sickness away."

> Behold the proud, his soul is not upright in him;
> but the just shall live by his faith - Haba 2:4

We will live by our faith, or we will die by our lack of faith.

Choosing faith is choosing life.

Therefore, chose faith.

Say: "I reject fear and unbelief this year and chose faith. I reject worry and despair and choose hope. I will walk by faith, not by sight."

Faith is acting on the Word of God even when you're unsure of the physical results. It is taking action based on something God says or something He is saying in your heart, even if it's not making sense.

> *Faith doesn't always have to make sense. That's why it's faith. If it always makes complete sense before you do it, it's not faith.*

This year, God says, "Walk by faith, not by sight. Walk by faith, not by fear. Walk by faith, not by the news. That's how to be safe from the judgment determined for the earth."

Don't be carried away by any event or situation in your life or the world. Instead, pay attention to the Word and God's voice. God will always give you the right word, a word in and out of season. The Word may not come from the sky or come with charismatic rattling. It may not come from a special prophet.

On the contrary, the word may come while reading a book or listening to a sermon. It may come while you're meditating or singing.

If you make your heart ready and prepared, you will never lack the right words to guide you every time.

Whenever you sense the Word from God in your heart, believe it. Declare it, and follow it.

Ignore physical signs and stick with God's Word in your heart. That is faith - standing on a word from God. That is the key to walking in the supernatural.

PRAYERS

1. Heavenly Father, I thank You for Your Word. Today, I receive the Word of faith and surrender all my worries and fears to You. I declare that all things are possible for me this year. I can do all things through Christ, who gives me strength.

2. From now on, I give up all forms of unbelief that stop me from acting on the Word of God for my protection, health, and breakthrough. I declare that I am not under any evil oppression anymore. I am living in the Light, where darkness has no say.

3. This year, Father, open my heart to receive more of You daily. Keep me continually hungry

and thirsty for Your Word. Grant that my heart will remain open for the entrance of Thy Word and that my life will bring forth the fruits of faith, in the name of Jesus Christ.

4. From today, I command my senses, calculations, and reasonings to give way to faith in God's Word. I declare that my obedience and response to God's revealed Word will be swift, perfect, and without delay, in Jesus' name.

5. Henceforth, I declare my faith in the power of God and His Word. I believe in God's promises for my life. I know that God is faithful; His promises are Yea and Amen.

6. I re-commit myself to being invested in God's promises and holding onto them no matter what is happening physically, for I know that He that has promised is faithful.

7. This year, victory is mine every day. The Word of God will keep me and make me fruitful in every area of my life. I am unstoppable, in Jesus' name.

DECLARATIONS

1. By the authority of Jesus Christ, I declare that the power of Goliath is broken in my life.

2. I declare that fear and intimidation have no hold over me, for greater is He who is in me than he who is in the world.

3. I declare that my faith in God is unshakable, and I will not be moved by the giants that make themselves visible this year.

4. No weapon formed against me shall prosper, and every tongue that rises against me in judgment shall be condemned.

5. I am anointed by the Holy Spirit to overcome every obstacle and to walk in victory this year.

6. I am more than a conqueror through Christ who strengthens me.

7. I declare that God goes before me in every situation, and His presence surrounds me like a shield.

8. I have the mind of Christ, and I am equipped with divine wisdom and discernment, in Jesus' name.

9. I declare that the giants of oppression and darkness are dispelled from my life, in Jesus' name.

10. I am a warrior in God's army, and I march forward in the strength and authority of the LORD this year, in Jesus' name.

Amen.

DAY EIGHT

PROPHETIC WORD #8

THE YEAR OF NEW DREAMS AND SUPERNATURAL PROVISIONS

God is saying to you this year,

"My child, this is a year of new dreams, creative ideas, concepts, inventions, and supernatural provisions. The floodgates of heaven are opened upon the year. My faithful ones will be empowered with new thoughts and strategies for outstanding prosperity and success. Get ready to dream bigger than ever, for I will birth within you fresh visions and dreams that align with My purpose for you.

"Pay attention. A wave of new product ideas, solutions, and answers are blowing from above. Don't be stuck within your comfort zone. Don't be stuck with the known. Receive My whispers of innovation and be separated from the crowd this year. Be attentive to the nudging of My Spirit, and let into you My creative ideas that will revolutionize your circumstances. I am unlocking the door to new projects to showcase My glory and power through you.

"Receive the spirit of innovation, My child. I am the Creator, and I have placed within you the ability to bring forth new creations. Partner with Me in faith; you will see breakthroughs and advancements that will impact your life and the lives of others around you. I will take your dreams and works to new heights.

Remember, your source is Me, and earthly circumstances do not limit me. Do not be afraid to dream big. I am your Jehovah Jireh, and I will provide resources far more than enough to accomplish the dreams I give you. As you seek Me and step out in faith, expect supernatural provision in every area of your life. I will meet your needs according to My riches in glory, not according to the economy of your nation.

"Just as I provided manna in the desert and multiplied five loaves of bread and two fishes to feed five thousand men, women, and children, I will work miracles in your life. So, open your hands to receive from Me. Allow your mind to be a fertile ground for groundbreaking solutions and concepts. Step out of the box and allow your God-given gifts to flourish.

"Do not be discouraged by naysayers or roadblocks, for I am with you every step of the way. Remember, the most significant dreams are not born from logic but faith. So, trust in My direction, step into your calling, and unleash the seeds of value I am stirring in your spirit. This year, you will not only experience supernatural provision, but you will also become a source of provision for others.

APPLICATION

This year, position yourself to receive and steward new dreams, solutions, creative ideas, inventions, and supernatural provisions God is releasing. Ask God to unveil the dreams He has for you and to guide you in the works He has prepared in advance. Trust in His supernatural provision and be open to creative ideas that may stretch your faith and understanding.

Be intentional about cultivating an atmosphere of innovation in your life. Ask questions about solutions, the way forward, and not questions of regrets. Stay connected to the Holy Spirit, the ultimate source of creativity, and be willing to step out in faith as He leads you into new ventures and inventions. And don't forget that

God's ideas and solutions are not just for personal gain but to bring glory to Him and impact the world around you.

PRAYERS

1. Heavenly Father, thank You for declaring this a year of new dreams, creative ideas, inventions, and supernatural provisions. I declare that I am ready to receive and walk in the fullness of what You have for me this year. Empower me by Your Spirit to fulfill my divine purpose, in Jesus' name.

2. O LORD, I surrender my plans to You and ask for Your guidance in fulfilling the works You have prepared for me in advance. Open my eyes to see the dreams You have placed within my heart, and help me to position myself to receive and align with Your divine solutions this year, in Jesus' name.

3. Jehovah Jireh, my provider, thank You for being my provider throughout this new year. I break free from the chains of lack and limitation and enter a season of unlimited financial favor, in Jesus' name.

4. I declare that my mind is a fertile ground for creative ideas and revolutionary inventions this year. I surrender to the whispers of the Holy Spirit and declare that my God-given gifts will flourish and excel beyond human explanation, in the mighty name of Jesus Christ.

5. This year, I am a conduit of divine creativity, a pioneer in my field, and a pacesetter in the origination of solutions. My ideas, suggestions, and inventions will impact my company, career, community, and the world and bring glory to the name of the Lord, in Jesus' name.

6. This is my year to rise, shine, and impact the world for God's kingdom. I am a source of blessing and provision for others. I overcome every obstacle and naysayer with the power of faith and persistence, in Jesus' name.

7. Holy Spirit, inspire me with creative ideas that align with Your purpose for my life. Grant me the wisdom to bring forth concepts and designs that glorify Your name, in Jesus' name.

8. Holy Spirit, help me to be attentive to Your leading. Give me the courage to step into new ventures and innovations, and let Your glory be seen through my works, in Jesus' name.

9. I declare that this is the year of divine acceleration in my life. The Holy Spirit empowers my dreams and works and primes them to new heights. I walk supernatural breakthroughs in everything I do, in Jesus' name.

10. I declare that I enjoy abundant provision every day this year. I receive divine supplies in every area of my life. I receive the new dreams, ideas, and inventions God has ordained for me. My heart and plans are supernaturally aligned with His, in Jesus' name.

11. Holy Spirit, remove from me fear and hesitation and empower me to step into new realms of possibility. Use me to bring forth creations that make a positive impact in the lives of others, in Jesus' name.

MEDITATION

Ephesians 3:20 - Now to Him who is able to do exceedingly abundantly above all that we ask or think, according to the power that works in us (NKJV).

DAY NINE

PROPHETIC WORD #9

THE YEAR OF THE BLOOD INSURANCE

God is saying to you this year,

"Beloved, this is the year of *Divine Insurance* by the blood of Jesus. Just as the blood of Jesus secured redemption and salvation for all who believe, it also serves as a supernatural insurance policy that safeguards you from enemy attacks.

"This year, I am reminding you of the power and efficacy of the blood of Jesus. It is a divine seal that marks you as My child and grants you access to My protection. Place your faith in the blood of Jesus, not in the security systems of your government. I will surround you with a hedge of supernatural defense and preserve you from harm.

"Listen, My child, this will be a year of fear in the nations. The enemy will attack the lands and cause fear in the hearts of men. But do not be afraid. I have told you these things beforehand. Your victory and protection are sealed by the precious blood of Jesus Christ.

"This year, I am releasing a heightened awareness of the authority and triumph you possess through the blood of Jesus. Declare that you are more than a conqueror through Christ who loves you. The blood of Jesus speaks on your behalf and silences the enemy's accusations. The blood secures your position as an overcomer in every situation and assures you of victory.

"My child, do not underestimate the power of the blood. It is the weapon that disarms the enemy and releases breakthroughs. Use it to plead your case, to declare your victory, and to enforce your authority in the spirit realm.

"Apply the blood of Jesus over your life, loved ones, and possessions every day. As you do, you activate the divine insurance policy I provide. This insurance covers your physical and emotional health, relationships, finances, and every area of your life. No weapon formed against you shall prosper because the blood of Jesus prevails.

"Walk in the confident guarantee that comes from being covered by the blood of Jesus. Rest in the knowledge that you are secure and protected by the *ultimate insurance policy*— the blood of Jesus. Declare this as a year of *Divine Insurance* by the blood of Jesus. Let your heart experience the peace, security, and victory from His precious blood."

APPLICATION

Embrace the power of the blood of Jesus. Read and meditate on the significance of His blood shed for you. Declare the truth that it secures your redemption, forgiveness, and protection. Apply it daily in your life. Shout it. Sing it. Plead it. The blood is your undisputable covering shield against the attacks of the enemy.

Proclaim your authority through the blood of Jesus and enforce it in your circumstances. Stand firm against the enemy. Resist his tactics and temptations. The blood of Jesus disarms and defeats the enemy.

PRAYERS

1. Heavenly Father, thank You for the precious blood of Jesus that secures my redemption and protection. Today, I declare my faith in the power of the blood of Jesus and the divine insurance it provides for my life and family, in Jesus' name.

2. LORD Jesus Christ, thank You for shedding Your blood for me. Today and this year, I apply Your blood over my life, my family, my health, my relationships, and all that concerns me. Let Your blood serve as a covering and a shield against the attacks of the enemy.

3. I declare that I am more than a conqueror through Christ who loves me. I stand in the victory secured by the blood of Jesus. I reject fear, doubt, and every work of the enemy, knowing that His blood prevails over all, in Jesus' name.

4. In the name of Jesus Christ, I resist the devil and his devices. I stand firm in the authority I have through the blood of Jesus. I declare that no weapon formed against me shall prosper because the blood of Jesus protects me, in Jesus' name.

5. I apply the blood over my mind, emotions, and physical body. I declare healing and wholeness in every area of my being. By the blood of Jesus, I am restored and made whole, in Jesus' name.

6. Today, I claim the voice of the blood over my life, for the blood speaks a better word for and on my behalf. I nullify every accusation, attack, and assignment of the enemy through the voice and power of the blood of Jesus. There is no more condemnation against me, for the blood of Jesus is my defense, in Jesus' name.

7. By the blood of Jesus, I declare that this is a year of favor, breakthroughs, and open doors. I will not lack divine help, opportunities, and promotions. Goodness and mercy will follow me all the days of this year, in Jesus' name.

8. I declare that I am cloaked in Jesus' sacrifice, immune to the enemy's attacks, and secure in the Father's love. Sickness and misfortune are not my portion. Accidents, bloodshed, terror, and kidnapping, and not my lot, in Jesus' name.

9. At the end of this year, I will count everything connected to me, and none shall be missing, in Jesus' name.

8. Thank You, Father, for the power of the blood of Jesus. I rest in Your promises and trust in Your security and protection, in Jesus' name.

DECLARE THE BLOOD

1. By the Blood of Jesus Christ, I am redeemed from the power of sin and death (Eph. 1:7).

2. By the Blood of Jesus Christ, I am justified and made righteous before God (Rom. 5:9).

3. By the Blood of Jesus Christ, I am sanctified and set apart for God's purposes (Heb. 13:12).

4. By the Blood of Jesus Christ, I am forgiven of all my sins, past, present, and future (Col. 1:14).

5. By the Blood of Jesus Christ, I am cleansed from all unrighteousness (1 John 1:7).

6. By the Blood of Jesus Christ, I am a new creation; old things have passed away.

7. By the Blood of Jesus Christ, I am delivered from the kingdom of darkness (Col. 1:13).

8. By the Blood of Jesus Christ, I am translated into the kingdom of God's beloved Son.

9. By the Blood of Jesus Christ, I am healed, spirit, soul, and body (Isaiah 53:5).

10. By the Blood of Jesus Christ, I am free from every bondage and captivity (Gal. 5:1).

11. By the Blood of Jesus Christ, I am an overcomer, victorious in every situation.

12. By the Blood of Jesus Christ, I am protected from the enemy's attacks (Exodus 12:13).

13. By the Blood of Jesus Christ, I am covered and shielded from harm and danger.

14. By the Blood of Jesus Christ, I am established in peace.

15. By the Blood of Jesus Christ, I am blessed with every spiritual blessing in heavenly places (Ephesians 1:3).

16. By the Blood of Jesus Christ, I am an heir of God and a joint heir with Christ (Rom 8:17).

17. By the Blood of Jesus Christ, I am more than a conqueror (Romans 8:37).

18. By the Blood of Jesus Christ, I am filled with the Holy Spirit and empowered for service (Acts 1:8).

19. By the Blood of Jesus Christ, I am marked as a child of God, sealed for the day of redemption (Eph. 4:30)

20. By the Blood of Jesus Christ, I declare victory over every circumstance (Rev. 7:14).

MEDITATION

Revelation 12:11 - And they overcame him by the blood of the Lamb and by the word of their testimony, and they did not love their lives to the death (NKJV).

DAY TEN

PROPHETIC WORD #10

THE YEAR OF VICTORY OVER THE FORCES OF DARKNESS

God is saying to you this year,

"My child, arise and declare that this is your year of victory over the forces of darkness. In the past, they attacked, accused, oppressed, and manipulated you, but no more. I am taking back dominion in your life.

"Lift up your battle cry of triumph, for I have already won the war at Calvary! Where Satan meant evil against you, I will turn it around for your good. Every scheme of the enemy shall backfire this year. Those forces that have hindered your progress will flee in defeat. You have been anointed, equipped, and empowered to crush the head of the serpent under your feet. His power over your mind, will, emotions, and circumstances are declared over.

"Fear not, for greater is He in you than he that is in the world. Stride boldly in your identity and authority as an overcomer this year. Rise up as a warrior of light. Stand against the powers of darkness. You are not to fear or be intimidated.

"I am exposing the enemy's strategies and revealing his hidden schemes. I am giving you discernment and wisdom to recognize and counter his tactics effectively. I am releasing divine strategies and blueprints to dismantle the strongholds of darkness.

"Your prayers and declarations will release My power to demolish every barrier and obstacle the enemy has erected. You will see the manifestation of My victory in your life and the lives of those around you. No weapon formed against you shall prosper, and every tongue that rises against you in judgment stands condemned.

"My child, rise up in spiritual warfare and engage the enemy. Submit to Me and resist the devil; he will flee from you.

"Declare with confidence that generational curses are broken off your life and that you are blessed. Declare that the forces of witchcraft are destroyed and that you are untouchable. Declare that every evil altar and meeting against you and your family is overturned, and you are promoted. Declare that those who rise against you in one way scatter in seven different directions. This is a year of release and total deliverance. Declare, and I will confirm it."

APPLICATION

This is a year to rise in faith and take back what the enemy has stolen. Stand on the finished work of Calvary and decree victory over the forces of darkness—sickness, lack, confusion, delay, destruction, and all that exalts itself against the knowledge of Christ. Do not empower the enemy with your fear.

Identify specific areas of attack and battle in your life. Meditate on scriptures of victory and be transformed by renewing your mind. Wield the sword of the Spirit boldly and watch God turn every scheme of the enemy against itself to your advantage.

PRAYERS

1. Righteous Father, I arise today declaring that this is my year of complete victory over every demonic force of darkness. Satan and his legions have no power or dominion over me. I

break free from all bondages of the past and take back my life by the blood of Jesus.

2. LORD Jesus, thank You for crushing the head of the serpent at Calvary. I stand on the finished work and revoke all power, assignments, and schemes of the enemy against me, my family, and my possessions. Where the enemy meant evil, God, You will turn it around for my good, in Jesus' name.

3. Holy Spirit, help me walk circumspectly this year, discerning the wiles and deception of the enemy. Give me wisdom and revelation to dismantle every stronghold, undo every snare, and barricade myself by the blood of Jesus and the shield of Your faith, in Jesus' name.

4. In the name of Jesus Christ, I activate my keys of the kingdom to bind and loose, to decree and declare, to release and receive. I bind every spirit of infirmity, poverty, and fear

in my life, and I loose the spirit of health, wealth, and faith, in Jesus' name.

5. I release the fire of God to consume every work of the enemy in my life. I decree and declare that I am blessed, healed, and delivered. I receive the favor of God to manifest every promise of God, in Jesus' name.

6. I break off every generational curse of infirmity, sickness, poverty, dysfunction, addictions, and all manner of darkness over my life. I receive blessings, favor, increase, and every good thing from God the Father, in Jesus' name.

7. I command all demonic powers fuelling sickness in my body to leave now in the name of Jesus! Every affliction, disease, pain, and discomfort is destroyed. I receive perfect health and vitality.

8. I command the forces of witchcraft against my life and household to be destroyed by fire, in Jesus' name.

9. I place a supernatural arrest over any man or woman plotting against me and my family this year. I command them to be disbanded, banished, and never return, in Jesus' name.

10. Wherever darkness is gathering against me and my vision, I scatter it by the light and fire of the Holy Spirit. I declare that my path is illuminated with God's favor and breakthroughs in every area this year, in Jesus' matchless name.

MEDITATION

Luke 10:19 - Behold, I give unto you the power to tread on serpents and scorpions, and over all the power of the enemy: and nothing shall by any means hurt you (KJV).

DAY ELEVEN

PROPHETIC WORD #11

THE YEAR OF ROYALTY

God is saying to you this year,

"My child, you have endured much abuse and mistreatment at the hands of others, but no more, for I am placing a hedge of protection all around you. Like a royal child, you will dwell securely under the shadow of My wing.

"Any person who lifts their heel against you shall be cursed. I will repay them double for all the pain they cause. But you, My love, shall mount up with wings as eagles and soar into new realms of lifting and blessing.

"I have conferred upon you all the privileges of My righteousness, not because of who you are but because of who I am. You carry My very own bloodline, and as such, you deserve only the very best. You are royalty. This year, walk with your head held high, conduct yourself valiantly, and embrace your heavenly royalty.

"No longer will you tolerate abuse or mistreatment in any form. I am giving you the strength and courage to set healthy boundaries, speak up for yourself, and walk away from toxic relationships and situations. I am empowering you to break free from the cycle of abuse and to step into the freedom and dignity that I have destined for you.

This is a year I am turning the tables on your oppressors and bringing about a reckoning for the wrongs that have been done to you. Trust in My justice; I am the God who sees and will vindicate you.

"This is a year of walking in your true identity as a child of the King of kings. Embrace the inheritance and authority that is yours in Me. Live confidently, knowing you are loved, cherished, and protected by My angels. You are an overcomer, and nothing can diminish the value and purpose within you.

"Let the consciousness of who you are in Me saturate your being each day this year. Activate the dominion I have given you. Let this year mark the era where you leave behind every form of abuse to enter into all that I have predestined for you - unspeakable joy, peace, and a bright future.

"I am dressing you in a new garment of favor and distinction. For too long, you have walked in hand-me-downs and worn-out attire that does not truly reflect who you are in Christ. But no longer will you conform to the patterns of this world or allow your past to define you.

"I have specially designed a garment of many colors just for you. It fits you perfectly and brings out the radiance of My Spirit within you. This royal robe declares your position as My heir and co-heirs with Christ. Henceforth, move, think, and speak as one with royal blood.

"Wear this new garment with pride, confidence, and boldness. I have graced you with My beauty, ability, and anointing. I have made you pure, holy, and blameless. That's who you are.

APPLICATION

Beloved, take God at His word and arise from any place of victim mentality and abuse. Renounce all agreements with oppression and declare yourself royalty in Christ. See yourself as the LORD sees you - highly favored, fearfully, and wonderfully made.

Meditate on scriptures, reminding yourself you have dominion. Reflect on the benefits of Your new life in Christ and speak them in faith as a declaration. Speak life, peace, joy, and victory over every situation. Your words will establish God's truth and dismantle the enemy's lies.

Guard your heart and mind against distressing thoughts. Put on the new you that God sees. Discard every label, limitation, or false identity from your past. Let go of old mindsets, habits, and ungodly ties that hold you back. This is your time for a breakthrough.

PRAYERS

1. Heavenly Father, I receive Your specially designed garment of favor this year. Dress me in Your beauty, likeness, grace, and anointing. Help renew my mind and live out my new identity in You, in Jesus' name.

2. From now onwards, I pull off every old label, limitation, and false identity holding me back. I let go of mindsets, habits, and ties that are not pleasing to God. I declare that I am blessed, favored, empowered, and graced for a life of impact, in Jesus' name.

3. Today, I clothe myself with the belt of truth, the breastplate of righteousness, the shoes of peace, the shield of faith, the helmet of salvation, and the sword of the Spirit. I declare that I walk in God's unlimited grace, royalty, promotion, and position. I am anointed and empowered to bear fruits, in Jesus' name.

4. My Father, my Father, order my steps and cause me to walk in continual breakthrough and favor wherever I go this year, in the name of Jesus.

5. I declare that no more abuse, mistreatment, or attack can come near me from this day

forward. I dwell safely under the shadow of the Almighty, in Jesus' name.

6. I am a royal child. I see myself as God sees me - highly favored, fearfully, and wonderfully made, in Jesus' name.

7. I renounce all agreements with oppression, abuse, and victim mentality. I take authority over every work of darkness against my life. I decree that anyone who has lifted their heel against me is doubly cursed with their very own evil, in Jesus' name.

8. In the name of Jesus Christ, I activate a dominion mindset in me. I declare my victory over the works of the enemy.

9. This year, I enter the destiny God preordained for me. I will live with a royal mindset, walk in courage, unspeakable joy, and unequaled peace, in Jesus' name.

10. Thank You, Father. I receive this prophetic word of no more abuse and royalty with gratitude and faith. Thank You for the freedom and healing You are bringing into my life and the lives of others. May Your name be glorified, in Jesus' name.

MEDITATION

Isaiah 61:3 - *To console those who mourn in Zion, to give them beauty for ashes, the oil of joy for mourning, the garment of praise for the spirit of heaviness; that they may be called trees of righteousness, the planting of the LORD, that He may be glorified (NKJV).*

DAY TWELVE

PROPHETIC WORD #12

THE YEAR OF THE FAMILY

God is saying to you today,

"My beloved child, I see the longing within your soul, the yearning for deeper connections and meaningful relationships within your family. I remind you today that I am the God who planned the family system. I ordained it as a source of love, support, and growth. I declare to you that this is the Year of the Family.

"There is a supernatural stirring birthing restoration and healing in your family. Where there has been brokenness, I am releasing My mending touch. Where there has been strife and division, I am pouring out the oil of My peace. I am binding up wounds and rebuilding what has been torn down.

"Do not lose hope, for I am the God of miracles. I am turning the hearts of parents back to their children and children back to their parents. I am releasing a new surge of love and forgiveness, converting anger into compassion and resentment into grace.

"My child, continue to stand your ground as a catalyst for change within your family. You are a vessel of My love and reconciliation. Speak words of life and power. Declare restoration and grace. Communicate forgiveness and empathy. Demand the good and salvation of your loved ones.

"I am going before you to smooth out rough places and bring alignment to My design and vision for your household. Old wounds will be mended, and newfound joy will fill your home. "Where there was a lack, there will now be abundant provision. Your family will again operate as a tight-knit unit, understanding their functions and supporting one another. Marital love and trust will deepen, for I will impart wisdom from above. Children will blossom under virtuous mentoring.

"I will arrange supernatural encounters and appointments to bring about restoration and revolution. Trust in My timing, for I am working all things together for Your good. I who began a good work will complete it. Do your part and leave the rest for Me.

"In this Year of the Family, I am restoring natural families and birthing spiritual ones. I am aligning you with a band of believers who stand by you, supporting and encouraging you on your journey. Open your heart to receive the help I give you through your spiritual family.

"Rest assured that I have heard your cries, seen your tears, and acknowledged your heart's desires. Hold fast to the hope I have placed within you; I am faithful and will hasten My Word over your family to fulfil it.

APPLICATION

Receive this word in faith and declare supernatural turnaround over your family.

1. Prioritize family: Make a conscious decision to prioritize family this year. Invest time, effort, and resources into fostering solid bonds with your spouse, children, parents, and family members. Create space for quality time, open communication, and shared activities.

2. Preach love and forgiveness: Let go of past hurts and offenses and extend grace to one another. Encourage forgiveness of one another. This allows healing and restoration.

3. Lead spiritually: Take up your family's mantle of divine leadership. Become a servant-leader and cheer others on to unity. As much as possible, encouraging praying and studying the Word together, and model a life of submission to Christ.

4. Teach strong fundamentals: Be an example and teacher of kingdom values - trust, respect, and godliness. Teach your children the importance of honesty, focus, prayer, hard work, and righteousness. Emphasize the significance of honoring one another.

5. Be Patient: Show grace and patience to one another as you experience the challenges and imperfections of family life. Continue to pray and declare protection over your family. Bless in-laws, extended relations, and future spouses of children. Command blessings over your seed and their seed to a thousand generations. And continue to give thanks that this year kindles a fire of God's faithfulness through your lineage. Remember that each family member is a work in progress, and growth takes time.

PRAYERS

1. Heavenly Father, I thank You for the gift of family. I surrender my family to You and ask for Your guidance, wisdom, and grace. May Your love and peace reign in our midst this year, in the name of Jesus.

2. O LORD, I pray for the restoration and healing of broken relationships within my family. I release forgiveness and ask for Your supernatural reconciliation to take place. I bind the spirit of division and release the spirit of unity, in Jesus' name.

3. Father, help me to be a catalyst for positive change in my family. Teach and inspire me how to create an atmosphere of love, acceptance, and joy within my household. Strengthen the

bonds between family members, in Jesus' name.

4. Holy Spirit, empower me to lead my family spiritually. Give me the wisdom and patience to teach and guide my children in Your ways. Let Your presence be evident in our family life, in the name of Jesus.

5. Father, I pray for those longing for a family. Comfort them, surround them with Your love, and bring the right connections into their lives. Provide them with a family that will support and encourage them, in Jesus' name.

6. In the name of Jesus Christ, I declare that this is the Year of the Family. I declare unity, love, and restoration over my family. I release the power of forgiveness and grace over every family member. I declare healing, protection, and deliverance over me and my family, in Jesus' name.

7. I declare that my family is being saved and blessed by the power of God. I lift their names before heaven today. By faith, I release them into God's loving hands. I declare that the Holy Spirit is at work in their lives. He is touching their hearts, bringing conviction, and drawing them closer to Himself. Every chain of darkness is broken, and every spiritual and physical barrier is removed, in Jesus' name.

8. I declare that my family will step into the freedom found only in Christ, in Jesus' name.

9. I release divine appointments and encounters in the lives of my family members. I connect them with circumstances that will birth their deliverance and salvation, in Jesus' name.

10. I declare that God is faithful to His promises. I see favor, divine provision, and the goodness of God upon each member of my

family. God is restoring what was broken. He is healing what was wounded and bringing joy where there was sorrow. I will see the salvation of my family, in Jesus' name.

MEDITATION

Psalm 68:6 - God sets the solitary in families; He brings out those who are bound into prosperity, but the rebellious dwell in a dry land.

Psalm 133:1- Behold, how good and how pleasant it is for brethren to dwell together in unity!

Psalm 127:1 - Unless the Lord builds the house, they labor in vain who build it; unless the Lord guards the city, the watchman stays awake in vain.

DAY THIRTEEN

PROPHETIC WORD #13

THE YEAR OF RENEWING THE MIND

God is saying to you this year,

"My child, this is the Year of Renewing of the Mind. I am calling you to an intentional alteration where your thought patterns and perspectives align with My Word and My ways.

"I invite you to embark on a journey of training your mind, to shift your focus from the negative to the positive, from anxiety to peace, from doubt to faith. I have empowered you to take control of your thoughts and deliberately dwell on things that are good, Godly, noble, and praiseworthy.

"Remember this, My child: your mind is a battlefield, and the enemy seeks to plant seeds of fear, doubt, and negativity. But I have given you the power to overcome. Through the power of My Spirit and the truth of My Word, you can demolish every stronghold and take every thought captive to obey Christ.

"When you surrender your thoughts and align them with My Word, you will experience a revolution from the inside out. Your mind will become a sanctuary of holiness, where My wisdom, love, peace, and joy reside.

"Never underestimate the power of your thoughts. If you nurture thoughts of faith, hope, and love, you will reap a harvest of blessings and breakthroughs. But if you nurture thoughts of fear, anxiety, sadness, and failure, you will reap a harvest of confusion, depression, lack, and timidity. This is why I charge you to intentionally guard the gates of your mind, filter out negativity, and embrace positivity.

"Immerse yourself in My Word, for it is a lamp to your feet and a light to your path. Meditate on it day and night; allow it to permeate your thoughts and guide your decisions. My Word will renew your mind, reform your perspective, and align your desires with My will.

"My child, if you will listen to me and choose to train your mind this year, you will walk in greater clarity and discernment. I will open your eyes to see the opportunities and blessings surrounding you. I will reveal hidden truths and insights that will guide you on the path to success.

APPLICATION

1. Become intentional about renewing your mind because your mind is the gate into the spirit realm. Set aside dedicated time each day, create a quiet space where you can be alone with God, read His Word, and meditate on it.

2. Identify negative thought patterns and replace them with positive, uplifting thoughts. Whenever negative thoughts arise, focus on those aligned with God's Word and promises.

3. Memorize and meditate on Scripture verses that address areas where your mind needs renewal. Write them down and carry them with you, reciting them throughout the day.

4. Surround yourself with positive influences. Choose to spend time with people who encourage and inspire you. Engage in activities that uplift your spirit and contribute to renewing your mind.

5. Practice gratitude daily. Create a gratitude journal to record blessings and answered prayers. Take time each day to give thanks.

PRAYERS

1. Heavenly Father, I come before You in the name of Jesus, and I ask You to renew my mind. Help me align my thoughts with Your truth and cast down every harmful and destructive thought in me, in Jesus' name.

2. O LORD, I surrender my thoughts to You. Let Your Spirit transform my mind and bring every thought into obedience to Christ, in Jesus' name.

3. This year, I declare that I have the mind of Christ. I will think and see the world through His perspective, guided by love, wisdom, and understanding, in Jesus' name.

4. In the name of Jesus Christ, I renounce every lie and deception of the enemy that has taken

root in my mind. I break free from negative thought patterns and embrace the liberating power of the Word, in Jesus' name.

5. Holy Spirit, grant me discernment to recognize and reject thoughts contrary to Your will. Help me to filter out negativity and focus on what is good, true, and praiseworthy, in Jesus' name.

6. My Father, my Father, I thank You for the power of Your Word. Renew my mind as I read and meditate on it day and night this year. Change my philosophies and perspectives and align my mindset with Yours, in Jesus' name.

7. From today, I declare that my mind is a sanctuary of peace and joy. I cast out anxiety, fear, and doubt and replace them with faith, trust, and confidence, in Jesus' name.

8. Holy Spirit, grant me wisdom and clarity of thought in every decision. Cause my choices to align with Your perfect will, in Jesus' name.

9. Henceforth, I choose to nurture gratitude in my life. I choose to focus on God's goodness and faithfulness day and night. May thanksgiving overflow from my heart every day, in Jesus' name.

10. I declare that this is a Year of Renewing of the Mind, and I will experience all-round transformation, breakthroughs, and open doors, in Jesus' name.

MEDITATION

Romans 12:2 - Do not be conformed to this world, but be transformed by the renewal of your mind, that by testing you may discern what is the will of God, what is good and acceptable and perfect.

Philippians 4:8 - Finally, brothers and sisters, whatever is true, whatever is noble, whatever is right, whatever is pure, whatever is lovely, whatever is admirable—if anything is excellent or praiseworthy—think about such things.

2 Corinthians 10:5 - We demolish arguments and every pretension that sets itself up against the knowledge of God, and we take captive every thought to make it obedient to Christ.

DAY FOURTEEN

PROPHETIC WORD #14

THE YEAR OF REALIGNMENT

God is saying to you,

"My child, listen closely to My voice as I guide you in discerning the relationships and associations not aligned with My purposes for your life. I am calling you to break free from the yoke of ungodly alliances and partnerships that have entangled, misled, and held you back.

"A divine wind of separation and repositioning will blow in your life. I want to expose and dismantle ungodly partnerships, alliances, ties, and connections that hinder your growth and progress and keep you bound in cycles of defeat.

"I want you to know that before there will be lifting, there will be separation. Come out from every relationship that does not build you up, lead you to Me, and motivate you to a better life. Until you release and let go of those who need to be released and let go, you will not enter into the new doors I have opened for you.

"I want to bring new connections into your life. I want to realign you with equally beneficial relationships and partnerships. These alliances will bring forth fruitfulness and growth. They will challenge and encourage you towards a godly and prosperous life. They will empower your health and keep you in peace.

"I am repositioning you for greater impact and effectiveness. Allow Me to sever the ties that hold you back. Open your mouth and declare the removal of unholy alliances and partnerships from your life. Your declaration is your permission for My Spirit to work within you, through you, and for you. I will prune you and show you the…

Unhealthy relationships, such as toxic friendships, romantic connections, and family dynamics characterized by manipulation, control, and abuse.

Unhealthy habits, such as addictions, compulsive behaviors, and bad lifestyle choices detrimental to your physical, mental, and spiritual safety.

Unhealthy beliefs, such as restrictive thoughts, negative self-talk, and false views that limit your ability to reach your potential.

Unhealthy atmospheres, such as living or working environments that are physically, mentally, and spiritually poisonous.

Unhealthy spiritual influences, such as false teachings, spiritual manipulation, and subtle occult practices that hinder your receiving from Me.

"This is a year of untangling and purification, My child. Commit to walking with only those who draw you closer to Me. Set your heart to follow My instructions without compromise, and I will establish My authority fully in your life. Walk in the new freedom and wholeness that realignment with your destiny in Christ brings.

APPLICATION

In this year of breaking unholy alliances and realignment, it is crucial to align yourself with God's purposes and discern the relationships and connections that do not align with His will.

1. Seek God's guidance in discerning which alliances must be broken and realigned. Ask

Him to reveal any ungodly partnerships and associations that have hindered your growth and progress.

2. Don't be afraid to let go of unblessed ties and relationships. Look up to God to bring about a realignment in your life. Release any fears and insecurities that will hinder you from stepping into the new connections and partnerships God has for you.

3. Surrender all relationships and connections into God's hands. Ask Him to sever the ties that need to be broken and bring forth divine connections that will align with His purposes for your life.

4. Seek wisdom and guidance from the Holy Spirit in evaluating your current relationships, ties, and networks. Be willing to let go of any connections that need to go. Set boundaries where necessary, and be discerning regarding people you allow access into your life going forward.

PRAYERS

1. Heavenly Father, thank You for declaring this year as a year of breaking unholy alliances and soul ties - a year of realignment, new connections, and growth. I receive this word by faith and declare that so shall it be in my life, in Jesus' name.

2. O LORD, I surrender to the leading of Your Spirit in the realignment process. Open my eyes to see and understand soul ties that need to be severed. Sever any links that are not in line with Your will for me. Connect me with networks that will propel me into greater impact and effectiveness. Prune away what hinders my growth and liberty, in Jesus' name.

3. Father, I pray for healing and deliverance from past soul ties that have bound my heart.

Wash me with the cleansing power of the blood of Jesus Christ. Fill any voids in me with Your assurance. Baptize me with Your peace and joy, in Jesus' name.

4. Holy Spirit, I release the heaviness of past soul ties and unholy alliances today and claim perfect healing and restoration, in Jesus' name.

5. Thank You, Father, for breaking the chains that have hindered me. Open my heart to the divine realignment You have for me this year. Reposition me with those who will uplift and encourage me in my journey, in Jesus' name.

6. Holy Spirit, empower me to walk in obedience. When I am tempted to go back to my abusers and manipulators, hold me back by all means, in Jesus' name.

7. Holy Spirit, grant me the discernment to recognize godly and ungodly alliances. Open my eyes to see the relationships that need to be

broken and the connections that need to be embraced. Lead me in the path of divine alignments that will bring forth fruitfulness, in Jesus' name.

8. I come against the powers of fear, insecurity, and passivity that keep me bound to unholy alliances and soul ties. I declare that I am free from the chains of manipulation, control, and spiritual bondage, in Jesus' name.

9. I renounce and reject any agreements, covenants, or pacts made consciously or unconsciously with any evil spirits or ungodly influences. I command any demonic spirits assigned to enforce any unholy alliances in my life to be bound and rendered powerless, in Jesus' name.

10. I break every curse, spell, or voodoo placed upon me through unholy alliances and soul ties. I declare that my heart, mind, and soul are

cleansed with the precious blood of Jesus, in Jesus' name.

11. From today, I declare that no darkness can penetrate my life and spirit anymore. I am a child of God, filled with the Holy Spirit.

Thank You, Jesus!

MEDITATION

2 Corinthians 6:14 - Do not be yoked together with unbelievers. For what do righteousness and wickedness have in common? Or what fellowship can light have with darkness?

Galatians 5:1 - Stand fast in the liberty by which Christ has made us free, and do not be entangled again with a yoke of bondage.

DAY FIFTEEN

PROPHETIC WORD #15

THE YEAR OF THE DECLARER

God is saying to you this year,

"My child, I have called you to be a powerful declarer this year. Just as I spoke to Jeremiah, I am appointing you to uproot, tear down, build, and plant through the power of your declarations. Your words can shape and shift the spiritual atmosphere around you.

"I have empowered and given you authority to tread on snakes and scorpions. As you declare My Word in faith, heaven responds, and My kingdom is established on earth. I have given you the keys of the kingdom; whatever you bind on earth will be bound in heaven, and whatever you loose on earth will be loosed in heaven.

"I charge you, My child, to be a declarer this year. Speak to the mountains in your life, and they will be cast into the sea. Speak to the dry bones, and they will come alive. Call forth things that are not as though they are, for I am the God who gives life to the dead and calls into existence the things that do not exist.

"Let your declarations come from My Word. Meditate on My promises and speak them forth with authority. Prophesy life, healing, breakthrough, and restoration, and believe in the power of your declarations.

"You are already equipped with the spiritual authority to call forth visions, strategies, ideas, healings, and breakthroughs in your life, family, Church, and community. Even if circumstances around you look bleak, keep declaring life over dead situations, and you will see the breath of resurrection come forth. As you decree what I plant in your spirit, a valley of dry bones will transform into a vast, living army.

"Embrace the Year of the Declarer, and let your declarations resound. Step into the fullness of your authority as a believer. Speak forth My Word, and mighty things will manifest.

APPLICATION

Here are some practical ways to walk in this prophetic word:

1. Know the word: Study the Scriptures daily and feed your faith. There is a difference between a positive confession and a prophetic declaration. Positive confession is based on head knowledge, while prophetic declaration is based on declaring scriptures. It is important to establish your declarations on scriptural words and promises over your life and destiny.

2. Speak with faith and authority: Believe in the power of your declarations. Speak with confidence, knowing that your words can shift spiritual realities.

3. Declare healing and restoration: Declare healing and restoration over yourself and others. Declare freedom from bondage, deliverance from strongholds, and wholeness in body, soul, and spirit.

4. Prophesy life and hope: Speak life into every situation. Declare hope, joy, and peace over bleak or impossible circumstances.

5. Don't stop: Be persistent in declarations, even when you don't see immediate results. God is working behind the scenes, and His promises will surely come to pass.

PRAYERS

1. Heavenly Father, thank You for calling me to be a declarer this year. I surrender my words and my voice to You. Fill me with Your wisdom and revelation that my declarations may align with Your will and bring forth Your purposes in my life and on the earth, in Jesus' name.

2. Holy Spirit, guide me in declaring Your promises over my life and the lives of others this year. Help me to discern areas where declarations are needed. Grant me a deep understanding of Your Word that I may declare with power and effectiveness, in Jesus' name.

3. In the name of Jesus Christ, I receive the anointing to uproot, tear down, build, and plant through the power of my declarations. I declare that what is not of God in my life and family will be uprooted and destroyed, in Jesus' name.

4. I declare that I have a prophetic voice and a creative power. I have the authority to speak to the dry bones in my life and see them come to life. I declare this year to be the Year of the Declarer, a year to unleash my voice and speak with the authority of heaven, in Jesus' name.

5. I break the chains of silence and fear and receive a prophetic flow that dismantles strongholds and ignites transformation. My words are aligned with God's will and carry the weight of eternity and the power to reshape destinies.

6. I stand against doubt and negativity. I declare hope where despair lingers and life where death holds sway, in the name of Jesus.

7. From now on, my voice becomes a force of creation, reshaping the world around me and fulfilling the purposes of God. I now speak to the dry bones in my life. By the power of the

living God, I prophesy life, restoration, and a divine turnaround. I command the winds of the Holy Spirit to breathe into any areas of my life that are dead or dying. I speak to my health, marriage, relationship, ministry, children, and dreams. I command them to bring new life, vitality, breakthroughs, and abundance in Jesus' name.

8. I declare that, henceforth, I will not be discouraged by the appearance of desolation. I will not be moved by my sight. I will not be moved by things as they appear in the natural. I serve a God who brings beauty from ashes. His resurrection power is at work within me.

9. In the name of Jesus Christ, I arise with faith and speak to the mountains that stand before me. By the authority given to me, I command every obstacle and limitation to be cast into the sea, in Jesus' name.

10. I command the mountains of sickness, lack, debt, and stagnation to leave now and never return, in Jesus' name.

11. I speak to the mountains of unemployment, injustice, and death threatening to disappear. I speak to the mountains of endless quarrels, divorce threats, and strange women in my marriage to die by fire.

12. I speak to the mountains of delay, postponement, rejection, and abuse to dissolve and never appear again, in the name of Jesus, the Christ.

13. My words are spoken with faith and the will of God. Therefore, the mountains are dissolved forever and ever. I command breakthroughs, healings, and reconciliation to manifest in my life and family from now onwards, in Jesus' name.

MEDITATE

Mark 11:23 – *Truly I tell you, if anyone says to this mountain, 'Go, throw yourself into the sea,' and does not doubt in their heart but believes that what they say will happen, it will be done for them* (NIV).

DAY SIXTEEN

PROPHETIC WORD #16

THE YEAR OF ACCEPTABLE OFFERING AND HARVEST

"My beloved child, listen closely, for I declare that this is the Year of Acceptable Offering and Supernatural Harvest. As Abel offered a more excellent offering and pleased me, I want you to know that your giving speaks for you before Me. I hold your offerings as a pleasing aroma and store them in your account before Me. It's not just the coins clinking in church trays that I am talking about but the whispers of kindness sown in daily interactions, the moments of forgiveness gifted to those who trespass, and the sacrifices of time and energy poured into acts of love.

"I have seen your acts of generosity, and this is my commitment to you: *your seeds will bear fruits*. Every act of generosity, every seed sown, and every offering given with a willing heart cries out in the realms of the spirit and will become harvests in your life.

"I am a God who sees and remembers. I am faithful to My promises, and I will honor your obedience. Even now, I have prepared a harvest for you that will exceed your expectations and bring forth blessings beyond measure.

"But do not be tempted to rest on the past, for there is a rhythm to abundance. Just as Abel continued to tend his flock, offering the firstfruits of his labor, so must you remain faithful in your generosity. Let your present open-handedness flow like a bountiful spring, watering the soil of your future harvest.

"Resist the doubters, mockers, naysayers, and the subtle whisper of the enemy in your heart. When they say, *'Stop wasting your time, it doesn't matter,'* and try to discourage you, remind them of the mystery buried in a tiny seed. Every seed planted and nurtured in good soil grows to produce a great harvest.

"Remember, it is not the size of the seed or offering that matters, but the heart behind it. Every seed you sow today will yield a bountiful harvest tomorrow.

"And have you not heard? *'Give, and it will be given to you: good measure, pressed down, shaken together, and running over, will be poured into your lap. With the measure you use, it will be measured back to you.'* This is not a mere promise but a divine equation.

"Your generosity is a conduit for My blessings overflowing into your life in unexpected and abundant ways. Your offerings of faith, hope, and love transform lives, bring healing, and manifest My kingdom on the earth. Your generosity and willingness to give sacrificially reflect the image of My Son, Jesus Christ.

"So, do not grow weary or be discouraged. Your giving is not in vain. Every generosity, whether large or small, is significant in My eyes. Your offering is not measured solely by its monetary value but by the condition of your heart. Your giving is not limited to material possessions alone. Your time, talents, and resources are all valuable offerings before Me. As you sow them into My kingdom, I will multiply your seed and bring increase to every area of your life.

"Remember this also, My child, your giving is an act of praise and worship. It is a demonstration of your trust in Me. And I am committed to My Word: *I will not let your sacrifices go unrewarded.* So, step into this *Year of Acceptable Offering and Supernatural Harvest* with boldness and expectation. Receive the word by faith and allow it to ignite a fresh passion for giving within you. Embrace the joy of giving and watch heaven's floodgates open over you. I have spoken, and it shall come to pass.

APPLICATION

Reflect on past giving: Admit any doubts or discouragement you may have felt and surrender them to God. Thank Him for the opportunities you had to give in the past and ask Him to help you see how your past givings impacted others and brought glory to Him.

Purpose to remain generous: As you proceed in this *Year of Acceptable Offering and Supernatural Harvest*, determine to remain generous. Seek God's guidance on how to give sacrificially, not only in financial resources but also in your time, talents, and love. Ask Him to reveal areas of your life where you can sow and make a difference.

Be grateful: Continually express gratitude for the opportunity to give and be a blessing in the lives of others. Every time you give, be thankful. Cheerfulness and thankfulness are the rain that waters your giving.

Resist the doubters: Surrender any fears or doubts about giving to God. Let go of any connection that mocks the practice of giving and generosity. Pray to deepen your faith and know that God honors and rewards cheerful givers.

Generosity beyond finances: Acceptable offerings go beyond financial giving. Give your time, skills, and love to others in a way that reflects the heart of God. Continually look for opportunities to be a blessing.

PRAYERS

1. Heavenly Father, I thank You for the privilege of being a part of the divine rhythm of giving and receiving, sowing and reaping. As I get on with this year of acceptable offerings, grant me wisdom to discern Your leadership in my financial decisions. May my giving align with Your purposes and bring glory to Your name, in Jesus' name.

2. Father, I surrender my finances to You. Give me a cheerful and generous heart that finds joy in contributing to advancing Your kingdom. Let my giving bless others and a sweet fragrance before Your throne, in Jesus' name.

3. Holy Spirit, guide me in identifying areas where I can sow into kingdom expansion. Show me the opportunities to support missions,

ministries, and initiatives that align with Your heart. May my contributions impact the lives of those who need Your love and grace, in Jesus' name.

4. Father, I commit to prudent stewardship of the resources You have entrusted to me. Help me to manage my finances wisely, recognizing that I am a steward accountable to You. Grant me the discipline to be faithful in both small and large matters.

5. O LORD, open my eyes to opportunities for generosity beyond finances. Show me how to share my time, skills, and love with those around me. Use me as an instrument of Your kindness and compassion in the lives of others, in Jesus' name.

6. I declare that my giving is not in vain. As I sow acceptable offerings this year and beyond,

I receive supernatural harvests in every area of my life, in Jesus' name.

7. Heavenly Father, thank You for the assurance that You have seen and remembered my past givings. You are a rewarder of those who diligently seek You. As I continue to give with a willing heart, I receive the manifestation of Your supernatural harvest in my life, in Jesus' name.

8. God of the harvest, I thank You for the promises in Your Word. I receive by faith the bountiful harvest You have prepared for me in this year of acceptable offering. May Your blessings flow in every area of my life, and may I be a channel of Your generosity to others, in Jesus' name.

9. Thank You, Father, for the seeds sown through small and great acts of generosity over the years. I declare that I will always have more

than enough to give and live bountifully according to your riches in glory, in Jesus' name.

10. Holy Spirit, help me maintain an attitude of cheerful giving without weariness. Renew my strength to continue sowing faithfully both now and forever. I speak to the divine harvest winds and decree that they blow every seed I have planted to my destiny. Let increase, multiplication, and overflow characterize this season in my life, in Jesus' name.

11. I declare that I am an unashamed supporter of kingdom work. No one can discourage or stop me from giving. As I trust God with my seeds and resources, He brings increase and multiplication in my life, in Jesus' name.

MEDITATION

2 Corinthians 9: 6-8 - Remember this: Whoever sows sparingly will reap sparingly, and whoever sows generously will reap generously. ₇Each of you should give what you have decided in your heart to give, not reluctantly or under compulsion, for God loves a cheerful giver. ₈And God is able to bless you abundantly, so that in all things at all times, having all that you need, you will abound in every good work (NIV).

DAY SEVENTEEN

DECREE AND DECLARE

I TRUST IN YOU, O LORD!

1. In the name of Jesus Christ, I declare that I put my trust in You, O LORD, and not in my own power or might. You are the source of my strength and salvation (Zech 4:6).

2. I will not lean on my own understanding but acknowledge You in all my ways. You will direct my steps and make my paths straight (Prov. 3:5-6).

3. This year, I will seek Your will in everything I do, and You will show me the best way to go. You will guide me with Your eye and instruct me in the way I should go (Psalm 32:8).

4. I declare I will not walk in the way of sinners or in the path of the scornful. With the help of the Holy Spirit, I will turn away from sin and walk in holiness (1 John 1:9).

5. I will trust in the Lord and do good. I will commit all my ways to Him, delight myself in His ways, and He will bring to pass the desires of my heart (Psalm 37:3-4).

6. In the name of Jesus Christ, my mind will stay on You, O LORD, and You will keep me in perfect peace. You will uphold me with Your righteous right hand and deliver me from every evil (Isaiah 26:3, Isaiah 41:10).

7. This year, I will not trust in the arm of flesh, but in You, the living God. You are my refuge and my fortress, my God, whom I trust. You will deliver me from every trap and protect me from every danger (Jeremiah 17:5).

8. This year, I will be like a tree planted by the waters, spreading out and flourishing at all times. I will not fear when heat comes; I will be evergreen and fruitful. I will not be nervous in the year of drought; I will prosper in everything I lay my hands to do (Jer. 17:7-8).

9. I will not labor in vain or spend my strength for nothing. You, O Lord, will bless the work of my hands and increase the fruit of my womb. You will make me the head and not the tail, above and not beneath, in Jesus' name.

10. I declare that I will seek first the kingdom of God and His righteousness, and He will add everything I need to me. He will supply all my needs according to His riches in glory by Christ Jesus. He will open the windows of heaven and pour out a blessing that I will not have room enough to receive, in Jesus' name (Matt 6:33).

I SHALL LIVE AND NOT DIE

1. Thank You, Heavenly Father, for the promise of long life to those who obey You. I praise and magnify Your name now and forever, in Jesus' name (Psalm 92:14).

2. O LORD, help me walk in Your ways and keep Your instructions. Plant Your laws in my heart and help me never forget them. May they lengthen my days and bring peace and security to me and my home, in Jesus' name (Proverbs 3:1-2)

3. I decree that my life is hidden in Christ. I am protected from the power of death. The blood of Jesus covers me. No weapon of death formed against me shall prosper, in Jesus' name (Colossians 3:3).

4. I declare that I shall live and not die, for God will satisfy me with long life and show me His salvation, in Jesus' name (Psalm 91:16)

5. I reject the spirit of death and declare that premature death is not part of God's plans for me. I will live a long, healthy life (Proverbs 3:1-2, Proverbs 18:21).

6. I commit my life to God's hands. Holy Spirit, engrave the fear of God in my heart and cause my obedience to prolong my days, in Jesus' name (Job 36:11, Proverbs 10:27).

7. I declare that no member of my family shall die prematurely. I rebuke and bind the spirit of death over my life, family, and loved ones. There will be no sorrow, mourning, or premature funerals in my family this year. We will fulfill the number of our years, in Jesus' mighty name (Isaiah 65:23).

8. I pronounce longevity, strength, and vitality over my physical body, soul, and spirit. I cover myself and my family with the blood of Jesus, in Jesus' name (Revelation 12:11).

9. My trust is in the LORD God Almighty. He satisfies me with a long life, and I find refuge under His wings (Psalm 91:16).

10. Thank You, LORD, for the assurance of long life and divine protection. I declare that my years shall be filled with joy, prosperity, and the manifestation of Your goodness, in Jesus' mighty name.

THE RESURRECTION POWER IS AT WORK IN ME; I AM SEATED ABOVE

1. This year, I decree and declare that by the resurrection power of Jesus Christ, I am set free from the power of sin and death (Ro.8:2).

2. By the resurrection power of Jesus Christ, every obstacle at the edge of my rising is removed (Matthew 28:2-4).

3. By the resurrection power of Jesus Christ, I am filled with hope and peace that transcends circumstances (1 Peter 1:3).

4. By the resurrection power of Jesus Christ, I am empowered to walk in victory over every challenge (1 Corinthians 15:57).

5. By the resurrection power of Jesus Christ, I am renewed in my mind, heart, and spirit (Romans 12:2).

6. By the resurrection power of Jesus Christ, I overcome every attack, trial, and test set against me (Colossians 2:15).

7. By the resurrection power of Jesus Christ, I receive wisdom, favor, grace, and energy to be an agent of transformation (Phil 3:10).

8. By the resurrection power of Jesus Christ, I receive boldness, confidence, and courage to excel in life (Philippians 4:13).

9. By the resurrection power of Jesus Christ, I am healed and restored, body, soul, and spirit (1 Peter 2:24).

10. By the resurrection power of Jesus Christ, I receive grace to live a life of purpose and destiny (2 Timothy 1:9).

11. By the resurrection power of Jesus Christ, I receive joy that cannot be shaken (John 16:22).

12. By the resurrection power of Jesus Christ, I am forgiven and washed clean by His precious blood (Ephesians 1:7).

13. By the resurrection power of Jesus Christ, I am embraced by the Father's love and acceptance (Romans 8:15).

14. By the resurrection power of Jesus Christ, I am an heir of eternal life and heavenly blessings (1 Peter 1:3-4).

15. By the resurrection power of Jesus Christ, I have become an instrument of grace and mercy to others (2 Corinthians 5:17).

16. By the resurrection power of Jesus Christ, I am anointed and equipped to fulfill my divine calling (1 John 2:20).

17. By the resurrection power of Jesus Christ, I am surrounded by angelic protection and provision this year (Psalm 91:11).

18. By the resurrection power of Jesus Christ, every dead dream and vision is coming back alive (Ezekiel 37:5-6).

19. By the resurrection power of Jesus Christ, I am strengthened and restored in spirit, soul, and body (Colossians 3:1-4).

20. By the resurrection power of Jesus Christ, I am sealed with the Holy Spirit, empowered for

service, and ready for His second coming (Ephesians 1:13-14).

COMMAND YOUR FINANCES

1. I decree and declare that in this new year, I am prosperous in everything I do, even as my soul prospers. I step into a year of all-around abundance and riches, in Jesus' name.

2. My barns are filled with plenty and overflowing with precious wines. I will lack no good thing, and I will have everything that makes life meaningful (Psalm 65:13).

3. I command every lost opportunity from the past year to come back to me in this new year. I decree restoration in every aspect of my life, in the name of Jesus (Joel 2:25).

4. In this new year, people I do not know will come and support me in rebuilding my walls,

and their kings will serve me. My gates will always stand open, and the wealth of the nations will come to me, in Jesus' name (Isaiah 60:11-12)

5. I declare that I am empowered to become an everlasting pride and joy to everyone. I will enjoy the prosperity of nations and dine with royalty, in Jesus' name (Isaiah 60:15-17)

6. I receive divine favor and abundance in this new year. I declare that I am blessed in health and wealth, and my gifts and skills open doors for me before kings and nobles, in Jesus' name (Proverbs 18:16).

7. From this day forward, my bosses, managers, colleagues, clients, and customers prefer me because my work and business are anointed, and the finger of God is upon me (Psalm 90:17).

8. I declare that I am empowered to lend to nations and will not borrow this year. The curse

of debt is broken off my life in the name of Jesus Christ (Deut. 28:12).

9. This year, nothing dies in my hands; I prosper in whatever I lay my hands on. The heavens are open to me, and I walk in supernatural prosperity all the days of my life, in Jesus' name (Deut 28:8).

10. I command financial increase and restoration to come into my life as I proceed into this year. I declare that I am supernaturally aligned with God's abundance and provision, in Jesus' name.

11. I will be a conduit of blessings and generosity this year. I will give and share with others and never lack, in Jesus' name (Psalm 68:19).

12. I declare that I carry a divine magnet that attracts favor for me this year. I prosper in

health, wealth, and relationships, in Jesus' name (Proverbs 3:4).

13. I declare that I will be divinely guided to opportunities that bring increase and success this year. I will walk in wisdom and discernment in my financial decisions, in Jesus' name (James 1:5).

14. As I progress into this new year, I break free from financial limitations and lack. I command miraculous supplies, wealth, and prosperity to manifest in my life, in Jesus' name (Gal. 5:1).

15. I declare that my financial breakthrough is this year. I release any fear or anxiety concerning my finances. God will bless me abundantly, in Jesus' name (Matt. 6:25-26).

16. I declare that my work and business are prosperous and blessed this year. I attract divine connections and strategic partnerships

for financial increase, in Jesus' name (Prov. 16:3)

17. I decree that I am a giver and a receiver. I am not a beggar. I sow seeds of generosity and reap a harvest of abundance. I am a blessing to others and will experience God's blessings in my life this year, in Jesus' name (2 Cor. 9:6).

18. I declare that my financial resources are multiplied this year. I will enjoy divine ideas and strategies to increase in wealth and impact, in Jesus' name (Ecclesiastes 5:19).

20. Thank You, LORD, for provision and abundance this year. I declare my trust in Your unfailing love and believe that You will meet all my financial needs according to Your riches in glory, in Jesus' name (Philippians 4:19).

COMMAND YOUR HEALTH

1. In the name of Jesus Christ, I declare that the LORD God Almighty forgives my sins and heals my diseases. He redeems my soul from destruction and crowns me with love and mercy (Psalm 103:2-4).

2. There is, therefore, no condemnation for me because I am in Christ. I have the confidence to appear before God and receive salvation, healing, deliverance, and restoration through the blood of Jesus Christ (Romans 8:1).

3. In the name of Jesus Christ, I exercise myself unto forgiveness and free my spirit from all hurts and offenses. I receive grace to walk in love and tolerance this year, in Jesus' name (Ephesians 4:32).

4. I forgive, not because I have been begged, but because I am a child of God. Even as the LORD has forgiven me, I also forgive anyone

who has offended me in the past, in Jesus' name (Matthew 6:14-15).

5. I receive deliverance from any bitterness and hurt from offenses of people. Whatever damage has been done to my health due to unforgiveness and anger, I receive total healing henceforth, in Jesus' name (Hebrews 12:15).

6. This year, I decree that I will be healthy, sound, and active in spirit, soul, and body. I will abound in love, grace, and peace, in Jesus' name (3 John 1:2).

7. Healing is the children's bread. I am a child of the LORD Jesus Christ, so healing is my portion. I see myself healed, renewed, and prosperous all through this year because that is the Will of God for my life, in Jesus' name (Matthew 15:26).

8. I reject pain and sickness this year. They are not part of God's plan for my life, in Jesus' name.

9. I declare that the hand of Christ is stretched towards me for complete cleansing and renewal this year, in Jesus' name (Jer. 33:6).

10. Jesus is the same yesterday, today, and forever. His love and compassion remain the same. This year, my family and I are beneficiaries of His mercy (Lam 3:22-23).

11. Because the compassion of the LORD fails not, our health will not fail this year, in Jesus' name (Lamentations 3:22).

12. I believe in the death and resurrection of Jesus Christ. He was wounded for my sins and chastised for my sickness. Therefore, I decree that I am healed forever and ever (1 Pet. 2:24).

13. No sickness has a right over my body because the blood of Jesus has redeemed me. My body is now the temple of the Holy Spirit (1 Cor. 6:19-20).

14. I command every form of sickness and pain in my body to be destroyed. I proclaim my healing and total restoration, in Jesus' name (Matthew 18:18).

15. God has given me authority over the devil and his demons through my faith in Christ Jesus. Whatever I bind on earth is bound in heaven, and whatever I loose remains loosed.

16. Today, I speak to the demons causing pain and sickness in my life and family. I bind them and command them to cease their operations, in Jesus' name (Mark 16:17).

17. I cast out every demon propagating sickness, pain, and weakness in my life and

family. I command them all to leave and never return, in Jesus' name (James 4:7).

18. I declare that I am seated with Christ in the heavenly places, far above principalities and powers. I rule with Christ as a king and priest before God (Ephesians 2:6).

19. I declare that I live in dominion over sin, sickness, and infirmities. The Blood of Jesus Christ creates a wall of protection over my life and family, in Jesus' name (1 John 4:4).

20. Throughout this year, I shall grow from strength to strength and from glory to glory, in Jesus' name (2 Corinthians 3:18).

PROPHESY OVER YOUR LIFE

1. This year, I declare that I can do all things through Christ who strengthens me.

2. my relationship with God grows deeper and deeper, and my love grows more and more until the perfect day.

3. I receive abundant grace to excel in the works of my hands and the power to walk in righteousness.

4. O Lord, set a guard over my mouth and watch over the door of my lips. Cause me to speak when necessary and make my words a token of healing and comfort for those who hear me this year, in Jesus' name (Pslm 141:3).

5. I declare that God's peace that passes understanding rules my heart this year. When storms arise in any way, my heart will be calm, my spirit will be at rest, and my access to divine order and instruction will be unshaken, for God is always with me. He will never leave me nor forsake me, in Jesus' name.

6. This year, I will walk in a manner worthy of the Lord, pleasing Him in all respects. I will bear abounding fruits of righteousness in every good work. I will increase in the knowledge of the Almighty.

7. I declare that God makes all grace abound toward me so that I always have all sufficiency and abundance in every good.

8. I declare that I am redeemed from all kinds of curses because Christ redeemed me from the curse of the law by becoming a curse for me. I enjoy all blessings as I serve and obey the Lord my God.

9. I will be blessed in the city and the country. I will be blessed in the fruit of my body. I will increase in my herds, cattle, and the offspring of my flock. I will be blessed when I come in and blessed when I go out.

10. I declare that any enemies who rise against me this year will be defeated before my face; when they come against me in one way, they will scatter before me in seven ways.

11. This year, all the people of the earth will see that I am called by the name of the LORD. I will be fruitful in the fruit of my body, in the increase of my livestock, and the produce of my ground. I will lend to others and will not borrow, in Jesus' name.

12. This year, the joy of the LORD will be my strength. There will be no depression, anxiety, and sorrow in my life, in Jesus' name.

13. God has redeemed my life from the pit. This year, He crowns me with His loving kindness and compassion. He satisfies my mouth with good things and renews my youth like the eagles' (Psalm 103:3-5).

14. Sadness, depression, frustration, and every other vice of the devil are far from me this year because the joy of the LORD is my strength. I will be still and see the salvation of God in every area of my life, in Jesus' name.

EPILOGUE

DECREE AND DECLARE

"God is at work in my life. Everything about me is getting better. When others are saying there's a casting down, I will be saying there's a lifting up. I am changing my world with my testimony because I am a shining light."

#Something Good Is On Your Way

GET IN TOUCH

We love testimonies.

We love to hear what God is doing worldwide as people draw close to Him in prayer.

Have you been blessed by this book or other books by me? Please share your story with us.

Also, please consider giving this book a review on Amazon and checking out our other titles at:

amazon.com/author/danielokpara .

Check out our website at www.BetterLifeWorld.org, and send your prayer request. God's power will manifest in your life as we join faith with you.

BOOKS BY THE SAME AUTHOR

Prayers to Cancel Disappointments at the Edge of Breakthrough

Prayers to Cancel the Curse of Marital Delay

Prayers to Remove Yourself from Negative Generational Patterns

31 Days in the School of Faith

31 Days With the Heroes of Faith

31 Days With the Holy Spirit

31 Days With Jesus

31 Days in the Parables

None of These Diseases

I Will Arise and Shine

Psalm 91

Prayer Retreat:
HEALING PRAYERS & CONFESSIONS
200 Violent Prayers
Hearing God's Voice in Painful Moments
Healing Prayers

Healing WORDS
Prayers That Break Curses
120 Powerful Night Prayers
How to Pray for Your Children Everyday
How to Pray for Your Family
Daily Prayer Guide
Make Him Respect You
How to Cast Out Demons from Your Home, Office & Property
Praying Through the Book of Psalms
The Students' Prayer Book
How to Pray and Receive Financial Miracle
Powerful Prayers to Destroy Witchcraft Attacks.
Deliverance from Marine Spirits
Deliverance From Python Spirit
Anger Management God's Way
How God Speaks to You
Deliverance of the Mind
20 Commonly Asked Questions About Demons
Praying the Promises of God
When God Is Silent
I SHALL NOT DIE

Praise Warfare
Prayers to Find a Godly Spouse
How to Exercise Authority Over Sickness
Under His Shadow

ABOUT THE AUTHOR

Daniel Chika Okpara's life assignment is to make lives better by teaching and preaching God's Word with signs and wonders. He is the resident pastor of Shining Light Christian Centre, a fast-growing church in Lagos. He is also the president and CEO of Better Life World Outreach Center, a non-denominational ministry dedicated to evangelism, prayer, and empowering God's people with the WORD and tools to make their lives better.

Daniel Okpara has authored over 100 life-transforming books and manuals on business, prayer, relationships, and victorious living, many of which have become best-sellers on Amazon and other bookstores.

He is a Computer Engineer by training and holds a master's degree in Christian Education from Continental Christian University. He is married, and they are blessed with lovely children.

WEBSITE: www.betterlifeworld.org

FREE BOOKS

To appreciate you obtaining this book, I'm offering you these four powerful books today for free. Download them on our website and take your relationship with God to a new level.

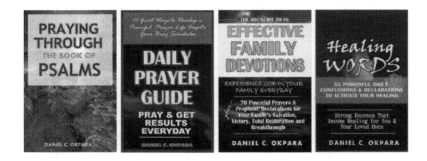

Click Here to Download

www.betterlifeworld.org/grow

NOTES

Manufactured by Amazon.ca
Bolton, ON

37787429R00125